for Patrick

MÁIRÍN DE BURCA:
Activist, Feminist, Socialist

With best Wishes

Máirín

BRIAN KENNY

GU00707486

MÁIRÍN DE BURCA
by Brian Kenny

Copyright ©2023 Brian Kenny

ALL RIGHTS RESERVED

ISBN 978-1-914488-94-8

Including the right of reproduction in whole or in part in any form.

Front Cover Photo: Máirín addressing a rally in Dublin's O'Connell St. c.1972.
De Burca archive.

Back Cover Photo: Mairin at 80. 2018. Photo: Derek Speirs

This edition printed and bound in the Republic of Ireland by

lettertec
Lettertec Publishing
Springhill House,
Carrigtwohill
Co. Cork
Republic of Ireland
www.selfpublishbooks.ie

For Máirín

Contents

Introduction

It is an honour to write the first full biography of Máirín De Burca.

During the two dramatic decades of the 1960s and the 1970s she was probably the most recognisable female political and social activist in the South of Ireland. She was a leading figure in Sinn Féin and, when that party split in two, in Official Sinn Féin. Through her political activity Máirín was involved in a whole range of social issues – housing action, women's liberation, prisoners' rights and international issues such as the Vietnam war and apartheid in South Africa.

She was a firebrand, a serial protestor and a frequent visitor to the courts. She served time in jail and was banned from visiting America. She was an internationalist and travelled to join with others in fighting for the rights of oppressed countries and peoples.

Capturing Máirín's varied career between one set of covers wasn't an easy task but it was certainly an enjoyable one. This book can best be described as an 'auto/biography.' At its centre are the many memories and accounts Máirín has of her life and work. These are supplemented in the more normal way by research, archive exploration, literature and newspaper review, and interviews with a number of her contemporaries.

Researching Máirín's life sometimes felt like being in the middle of a thriller novel. There were protests, evictions, bloody battles with the guards, court cases, sentences, appeals, jail time and more.

Máirín was very patient in answering all my many questions and requests for records and other information. She was, and is, unfailingly modest, often describing some dramatic protest or eviction with a simple 'that's what you did in those days'.

She was very clear with me in saying that as long as it was factually accurate I could write what I liked. Which I did. Having said that, it was hard to come across people she worked with who were negative and uncomplimentary about her. Not everyone thought Máirín was great - the guards she encountered in her many protests certainly didn't - but most people who knew her well admired her courage, her commitment and her fearlessness. And all of this bound up in her slight, 5 ft. 4 inches frame.

Máirín's direct, no nonsense way of dealing with the world was sometimes seen as off putting. Some people, often men, saw her as a woman to be afraid of or in awe of. But these same people had no hesitation in speaking also of how much they admired Máirín's passionate commitment to social justice and a peaceful Ireland.

Máirín De Burca's life and career is a story well worth telling, not only in itself but for what it tells us about how Ireland has evolved over the past seventy years. I can only hope I have done it justice.

Acknowledgements

Many people helped to bring this book to fruition. Firstly, of course, I want to thank Máirín for letting me into her life and allowing me to write about her. Her openness and cooperation made my job a very enjoyable one. So, thank you Máirín.

Secondly, I want to thank Tony Heffernan who suggested I write about Máirín and who helped in a number of ways, not least in raising finance towards the book's publication. I want to thank all those people for their generous financial contributions. This book would not have happened without them.

During September and October 2022 I interviewed a number of Máirín's former colleagues and contemporaries. Each of them was very generous with their time and in sharing their memories of Máirín.

So many thanks to:

Vincent Browne	Tony Heffernan
Pat Brennan	Pat Rabbitte
Rosheen Callender	Maurice Sheehan
Proinsias De Rossa	Rosita Sweetman
Des Geraghty	Padraig Yeates
Eamonn Farrell	

I also want to thank Aisling Dunlea from Trinity College library who helped me access a range of publications.

Thanks also to the staff of the National Library and the National Photographic Archive for their assistance in accessing documents and photographs.

As well as letting me interview him, Eamonn Farrell from Rolling News was of great assistance in accessing photo archives and in allowing me to use images from Rolling News. Derek Speirs, that great photo chronicler of protest in Ireland, made some of his photos available. In a similar vein I would like to thank Brenda Fitzsimons from *The Irish Times* for her assistance with photographs.

Eric Byrne, photographer supreme and former colleague of Máirín's, provided his technical expertise in preparing many of the photos for publication. Thank you, comrade. I also want to thank Michael 'the man who knows everything' O'Sullivan for his technical assistance with some photos.

Frank Murphy was very helpful in providing advice on the text.

As ever I want to thank Leonie O'Dowd for her ongoing support and her meticulous editorial skills. Thanks also to Fatema Mohammedi; I hope my efforts get me more than a C minus.

Notes on the text

Throughout the book I mainly use 'Máirín' rather than 'Máirín De Burca' or 'Ms. De Burca'. It fits with Máirín's informal and unfussy style. I also use 'the North' and 'the South' to describe both parts of the country. To describe the conflict in the North I use 'the Troubles'. And I mainly use 'the guards' to describe our men and women in blue.

With regard to Sinn Féin, when the party split into two organisations, I give the new entities their full titles - 'Official Sinn Féin' and 'Provisional Sinn Féin'. Their military wings were known as the 'Provisional IRA' and 'Official IRA, but I have mostly used the names they were better known by - 'the Provos' and 'the Officials'.

When quoting Máirín's own words from the interviews I conducted with her, I have used single quotation marks. For everything and everybody else it's double quotation marks.

Brian Kenny
May 2023

1. Beginnings

Imagine a three-year-old girl, living in one of America's biggest cities. She has just finished her first day at kindergarten but there is no one there to collect her. So she wanders around lost until eventually her mother appears. But the same thing happens the next day…

Roll forward a few years. The girl is six and going to primary school in the same big city. Her mother has to go into hospital to look after the little girl's brother and she warns her not to call into the neighbour's house after school. She wanders the streets for a few hours with a friend until her father returns from work. This goes on for a week. And somehow it's made clear to that young girl that she is a second class citizen and her parents really wanted a boy.

Imagine now the young girl is back living in rural Ireland. She's ten years old and it's 1948. What is she interested in? Her friends? Going around on her bike? Going to school? Probably all of the above, but what if she also wants to learn about the upcoming General Election and she studies *The Irish Independent* to learn what this politics stuff is all about?

And then there's the family rosary. She's still a young girl, maybe ten or eleven, but kneeling every evening to say the rosary doesn't feel right. So one night the others kneel and she stays sitting. Nobody says anything but another barrier has been broken.

The girl becomes a teenager, still living in rural Ireland in the 1950s. Her father tells the family a story about a black man who was refused a drink in a bar in Chicago. He is pleased. Without thinking she says 'If I was there I would have walked out with him.' Everyone looks at her as if she has two heads, but she doesn't back down. Then, as soon as she's sixteen, she joins a political party where she cycles home from meetings on her own in the dead of night.

And so, the long journey begins. Máirín De Burca grew up to be an independent, resilient feminist and a committed social and political activist … we should not be surprised.

2. From Chicago To Newbridge

From her early childhood years Máirín De Burca was independent; it was something she had to learn. She was born in January 1938 to Molly Farrell, from Newbridge, County Kildare and Patrick Burke from Gort, County Galway. Máirín was the second child and spent the first nine years of her life in America. Her parents had met initially in Ireland, coincidentally at a Sinn Féin dance, and then emigrated separately to Chicago where they reunited. They married in the 1930s and had their first child Patrick who died in tragic circumstances when he was six years old.

Molly Farrell/Burke had returned to Ireland to sort out a family will, and young Patrick stayed at home with his father. Patrick was then sent to Ireland with a friend to be reunited with his mother. Tragically, he contracted pneumonia on the long ship journey and died soon afterwards. It was a cruel blow and one from which his parents never fully recovered.

Máirín came along after Patrick died and in a later interview recalled that "In many ways it set the tone for the rest of their lives; it broke their hearts, both of them. There would be days when my father wouldn't be speaking to anybody. It could have been Patrick's birthday, his anniversary."[1] Patrick's death remained with his sister Máirín who sadly noted that she would "go to my grave not knowing where my brother that died is buried."[2] This tragic event undoubtedly had an impact on Máirín although she looks back on her childhood as being positive in many respects.

Mary Margaret Burke

By 1937 Molly was pregnant again and she returned to Ireland from Chicago so that she could give birth in her hometown of Newbridge. Mary Margaret Burke was born on the 8th of January 1938 and soon became known as Máirín. Patrick had died at this stage and Máirín's parents had wanted another boy. From an early stage it was clear to Máirín that she was looked on as a 'second class citizen'.

Back in Chicago Máirín started kindergarten at the age of three. In a short article/memoir she wrote many years later Máirín recalled her mother decided "that before I went (to school) I should be able to read simple children's books and do simple addition and subtraction … I was the infant prodigy of the Convent of the Sacred Heart in Chicago."[3]

That learning was of no use to Máirín at the end of her first day in kindergarten. 'The war was on and in a fit of patriotism the nuns played a Sousa march and got us

---

1   Documentary film by Cathal Black – *A Loner's Instinct* (Nightingale Films, 2019)
2   *The Irish Times, The Women's Podcast Episode 294,* 28th March 2019
3   *The Irish Times* (Education Supplement), 7th May 1972

all to line up in North, South, East and West lines. I was three years old and had no idea what direction I lived in and on the first two days I picked the wrong direction and got lost. I was frantic but my mother eventually found me. By the third day I found out the direction and walked home safely.' It appears that three-year-old children walking home from kindergarten was not uncommon in 1930s Chicago. Máirín was learning that she had to grow up fast.

3-year-old Máirín goes 'horse riding' in Chicago.
De Burca archive.

When Máirín was seven she made her first communion and again she was on her own. 'Mammy put me in my white dress and veil, put me out the door and closed it behind me. One of our neighbours saw me on my own at the church and pushed an envelope into my hand. When the ceremony was over, I ran home and that was it.' When my brother had his communion things were different. 'Daddy took a day off work and after the ceremony we went for a drive and a meal. To this day that annoys me.'

In 1930s America it was no surprise that Molly Burke was a 'stay at home' mother, but it didn't suit her. 'Mother didn't work in Chicago, although she would have liked to. Daddy was an old-fashioned man and if your wife worked it meant you weren't able to look after her.' The fact that Molly couldn't work did impact on family life. 'She would have loved to work and have her own money. She liked doing things. She didn't like staying around the house. She didn't have a life of her own. We would have been a happier family if she had worked.'

Brother Michael

Sometime after Máirín was born a new brother, Michael, arrived into the Burke household. The circumstances were never explained fully but Máirín believes that Michael was one of triplets and was given to her parents or possibly adopted. The important thing for Máirín's parents was that Michael was a boy.

Chicago in the 1930s and during the Second World War was difficult and Máirín's father spent many days tramping the streets looking for work. Eventually he found employment as a carpenter in the Marshall Field building and stayed there until his retirement.

The Burkes were proud Irish Catholics and regarded others, even other Irish, as inferior. It was often a case of one nationality looking down on another. "There was a distinct hostility on the part of Germans in Chicago to the Irish, which I can only now put down to the antipathy the Irish displayed to anyone who wasn't Irish."[4] Máirín's parents were particularly derogatory in the way they spoke about black people.

There was politics in the Burke household with Máirín's father a keen supporter of the IRA. Máirín's aunt, also living in Chicago, was interested in politics as well and Máirín's father had regular arguments with her about the respective merits of the Republican and Democrat parties.[5] Patrick Burke was both an Irish republican and, in America, a Republican with a capital R. He supported the Republican party primarily because it didn't agree with America entering the Second World War to assist the British. These family debates were lively and somehow they seeped into Máirín's consciousness.

---

4   Ibid.
5   *The Irish Times* Women's Podcast, No. 294.

School Days

Primary school in Chicago was enjoyable and Máirín got on well at her studies. The school was co-educational and there was no corporal punishment. There was, however, religion and plenty of it. Prayers were said "at every conceivable occasion … we attended retreats, benedictions and sodalities; we had daily visits from priests and periodic visits from nuns."[6] It sounded just like Ireland.

Máirín made friends easily, a trait she was able to continue through her life. Similar to her experience in kindergarten, she had been warned by her mother that if she was out when Máirín returned home from school, she was never to go into their landlord's home and shop, which was on the ground floor of the house where they lived. This family were also Irish and would have been happy to mind her.

On one occasion Michael fell ill and his mother took him to hospital. 'She didn't come home until six days later. I couldn't get back into the flat until Daddy came home and I was forbidden from asking the friendly Irish couple who owned the house to let me in or to accept any food from them. I had to walk around for about three hours …no one gave a shit about me quite frankly… It never occurred to Daddy to take a week off work. It was a clear indication of my standing in the family. At the time

---

6   *The Irish Times*, 7th May 1972

I accepted it as normal. My mother didn't want to be beholden. Irish country people are like that.'

Despite these difficulties Máirín recalled in her article on her school years that "Anyone who is reading this to enjoy another of those grinding, harrowing stories of hated schooldays better skip it. I was very happy indeed at school."[7]

Black People

Máirín's independence and opposition to people being badly treated surfaced at an early age. While cycling her tricycle around the streets of Chicago one day a black woman called Máirín over, pointed out a penny on the ground and told her to take it. Despite Máirín's reservations, the woman insisted she take the penny. This generous gesture did not accord in Máirín's young mind with the message she was receiving at home about black people.

Some years later, back in Ireland, Máirín was able to challenge her father's attitudes. He had told the family a story about coming home one night from the pub in America where a black man had been refused a drink. Máirín's father was very bigoted against black people. "Daddy was really pleased but I said 'If I had been there Daddy I would have walked out with him'.… Everyone looked at me as if I had two heads… I lay awake for ages

---

7   Ibid.

that night thinking – 'Where did that come from.' I had no opinion of black versus white people whatsoever. I just thought… the injustice of it."[8]

Máirín aged 9, with her parents and brother Michael before the family returns to Ireland. De Burca archive.

For Máirín's parents Chicago was always going to be a temporary home. They rented a variety of apartments and houses with Patrick Burke always opposed to the permanency of buying a house. With the end of the

---

8   *The Better Side Podcast* – Aodhán O'Riordain, Near FM, !4th February 2017

Second World War the Burke family were keen to get back to Ireland. However, they had to wait until October 1947 when the seas had been cleared of mines and it was safe to leave. Molly Burke sailed first to Cobh with Máirín and Michael. Husband Patrick staying behind in his secure job, remaining in Chicago until his retirement in 1951.

Apart from the occasional visit, Máirín didn't see her father for over three years but she didn't miss him. 'Daddy staying back in the US didn't affect me in the slightest. Daddy and I had little interaction. To be fair it was the same between Daddy and Michael. I think Daddy couldn't interact with a girl and, grieving for his son, wasn't able to love an adoptee.'

Newbridge

Máirín's mother couldn't wait to get back to Scarletstown, an area a few kilometres from Newbridge, where she grew up on the family farm. 'I think my mother had a really happy childhood there, she always referred to it in happy terms.'

Máirín's father had hoped to return to his home county of Galway and had ambitions to open a pub there when he retired. In the end Newbridge won out and Molly moved there with the two children, initially staying with some of Molly's relatives. The Burkes subsequently built a modest two-bedroom house, located two miles outside

Newbridge. Nine-year-old Máirín was delighted with the move. She remembers vividly 'that on the first morning after our arrival I looked out the window to see a cow pressed up against it. I was so excited that I thought I had gone to heaven.'

Máirín liked school where she was educated in her mother's old school, the Convent of Mary Immaculate in nearby Newbridge. On the first day at school her mother told the teacher she wouldn't be doing Irish, which was not Máirín's decision. This was a choice which Máirín 'forever after regretted' as she then wasn't able to sit any subsequent state exams. Despite this setback Máirín liked to study and focused on subjects like English which she particularly enjoyed.

Corporal Punishment

In her Irish school Máirín now had to adjust to losing what she described as "her immunity from 'capital punishment'. I was walloped like the rest of them and no doubt my utter dislike for authority can be traced to this stage."[9] Unfortunately for Máirín "education wasn't important in our house and you were expected to leave the minute you could."[10]

As she wasn't studying Irish and couldn't take state exams Máirín was left to her own devices. She was in fact

---

9   ibid
10 *The Irish Times, The Women's Podcast*

ignored and could study or not as she decided. "I could learn or not as the whim took me... No one tried to cram subjects into me or worried if I stayed out of school. The result of this was that I never stayed away if I could help it. I learned just those things that interested me, and I left at 13 with relief on the part of the nuns and pleasant memories of mine."[11]

In marked contrast Máirín's brother Michael, who was four years older, never went to school when the family returned home. He was twelve at the time and his mother's undoubted favourite. Michael 'had definite psychological problems... He used get sick at the thought of going to school; he was afraid he wouldn't be able to answer the questions... he dropped out of school at the age of twelve. He was smothered.' That was certainly something Máirín never experienced.

Writing when she was thirty-four, Máirín's overall reflection on school was, "I have now nothing that I took away from school...except my anarchism... I completely exonerate the nuns of any of my three schools from any responsibility whatever for my behaviour after I left school... the best compliment I could pay them is to say with sincere thanks 'I got it early and rejected it before it seriously affected my life.'"[12]

---

11   *The Irish Times*, 7th May 1972
12   Ibid

A Girl Alone

Whether she liked it or not Máirín had to learn to be independent throughout her school going years. 'I was very much left on my own… girls in our family … people weren't interested, so you kind of got on with it. Rearing yourself, making your own plans and deciding yourself what you wanted to do… I'm not complaining, this is how it was and perhaps it stood to me.' Despite having no complaints about her school years, it is not surprising that many years later Máirín recalled that she "must have been the only child in Newbridge who wanted to go to boarding school so that I could get away from my dear family."[13]

Máirín was a keen reader and was very excited when she became old enough to join the local library. 'I dashed home to get Mammy to sign the form, but she wouldn't do it. She said if you get books you will do nothing, you will sit in the corner reading all the time. I went to bed and cried all night.' The next day a long faced Máirín explained her woes to a friend. She promptly brought her home at lunchtime and the girl's mother signed the form. Thereafter 'I came home with books two or three times a week and my mother never asked me how I got my card. It was a lesson for me – you never ask, you do.'

There were many good sides to living back in Ireland. There was a freedom in rural Kildare that Chicago could never match. Máirín had two girl cousins living

---

13   *The Irish Times*, 3ʳᵈ December, 1975

nearby. 'We were close, and they were the nearest I had to sisters. We palled around and on fine weekends we'd get on our bikes and take off for the day, all round the roads of Kildare.' Even a trip to Glendalough, a distance of over forty kilometres, wasn't beyond them. And with the innocence of youth and of the times, they were sometimes able to hitch a lift from a farmer passing with his trailer when the going got too hard.

Politics and Work

As a staunch Catholic family, Sunday mass and evening rosary were all part of the weekly ritual. Máirín disliked the rosary in particular and agonised for a week until one night she didn't kneel for it and instead sat in her chair. That was it and she was never challenged. An important lesson for Máirín in having courage and also realising that outcomes often aren't as bad as you fear.

Máirín was always interested in the world around her. In 1948, a year after she came home, a General Election was called when Taoiseach Eamon De Valera sought a new mandate. Ten-year-old Máirín decided she wanted to know more. 'I wanted to understand what it was all about. I read all their speeches in the *Irish Independent*. I couldn't make sense of it but it did light a fuse.'

However, Máirín knew that her father was a great admirer of De Valera and her father believed "that Ireland began and stopped with Dev. And I thought it too… in the '48

21

election I nearly broke my heart when he (De Valera) didn't win."[14] Many years later she was to come across De Valera in a very different set of circumstances.

Constant Reading

What also lit a fuse for Máirín was her constant reading. As the library in Newbridge opened irregularly, she used to pick the largest books. One of these was about the Young Irelanders, a group of young men who launched a failed rebellion in 1848. Reading the exploits of these youthful rebels was a lightbulb moment for Máirín and convinced her to join Sinn Féin as soon as she could.[15]

Up to then Máirín had decided she was going to be a nun. "I had picked out the Order – The Missionary Sisters of Saint Columban – I was really attracted to the Missions, working outdoors in the fields."[16] Perhaps luckily for The Missions they had to wait and at the age of thirteen Máirín left school and got a job as a shop assistant in Hederman's Drapers in Newbridge. By her own admission she wasn't very good at it. In a later interview Máirín claimed that she "was the worst shop assistant in the world because she hate(d) dealing with people."[17] Her attitude was not helped by being paid five shillings for sixty plus hours per week which included many late

---

14 *Irish Press,* 29th January 1970
15 ibid
16 *The Other Side* Podcast
17 Anne Stopper- *Monday's at Gaj's: The Story of the Irish Women's Liberation Movement,* ch. 2 (The Liffey Press, 2006)

nights. One Christmas Eve the shop had stayed open late to facilitate the farmers.[18] Máirín didn't get to leave until 11.30 pm, meeting people heading to midnight Mass on her way home.

Sinn Féin

Máirín's political views continued to develop and in her early teens she tried to join Sinn Féin but was told she was too young. As soon as she was sixteen she was old enough and she enlisted in the local cumann (a local branch of the party). Her reason for joining was straightforward - 'A united Ireland. It was their only aim and objective, it was as simple as that. The other parties didn't mention it that much, if at all.'

One of her first political activities was selling Easter Lilies to raise funds for Irish prisoners in England. "The person sitting next to me was a well-known member of Fine Gael, Christy Moore's father, Andy. Weird, wasn't it?"[19] There were occasional cumann meetings to attend which often started late. Máirín would be out into the early hours, cycling home in the dark but without her parents worrying where their teenage girl had got to.

Having worked in Newbridge for two years, Máirín was ready to spread her wings. She didn't feel that her political interests could be met in Newbridge. Apart from

---

18 ibid
19 *The Other Side* Podcast

that she had a very clear desire for greater independence. "The main ambition of my youth was to leave home and be totally alone and independent. That was a real need, not just an ambition."[20]

In 1954 Máirín secured a new job in Bray, County Wicklow. It was with Tansey's drapers and the pay wasn't much more than five shillings per week, but she had her own 'digs', she was on her own and was now able to get fully involved politically. The day she was leaving for Bray her mother called her aside. 'With dread I followed her. Was this going to be the facts of life lecture? It wasn't and instead she ended up giving me a warning – keep your politics to yourself.' Máirín's mother was going to be disappointed.

20   Ibid

3. Sinn Féin By The Sea

Bray was different. Máirín was now away from home and living on her own. It was another retail job ;the work wasn't exciting, and the pay wasn't great, but Máirín was independent with the freedom to pursue her various interests.

She was a sociable girl and Bray gave her an opportunity to get out into the world. 'I liked dancing and one night I went to a dance in Greystones and everyone else was in couples except myself and three other girls. We got chatting and even though we got no dances we became lifelong friends.' Máirín particularly loved céilí dancing and went to every céilí that was on.

Sociable Loner

In Bray, Máirín developed 'a wonderful group of women friends and we would meet in each other's houses, go on picnics and hikes. We went to the Abbey theatre a lot and a picture house (in Dublin which) … showed foreign films which were really exotic for us then.' Máirín also joined the local amateur drama group and on one occasion found herself playing a leading role in *The Last of Summer* by Kate O'Brien. (When Máirín's landlady heard about the play she whispered to her, 'She (O'Brien) was only married for twenty-four hours, you know.' Kate O'Brien was a lesbian woman who had two of her novels banned.)

Máirín and Peggy Doyle, her work colleague from Tansey's shop. c. 1956. De Burca archive.

Through her acting, Máirín was introduced to Micheál Mac Liammóir. Máirín was excited but nervous and brought along her copy of his autobiography 'All For Hecuba' for him to sign. 'I was terribly shy, starstruck. My friend told him I was shy and in his grand voice Mac Liammóir replied. 'Is she shy? So am I', then shook my hand and signed the book.'

While she was sociable, Máirín liked the idea of being able to go home alone and close the door behind her. This trait began when she was a teenager and continued throughout her life. Máirín continued to be a keen reader and one of the first things she did in Bray was join the local library and this time she didn't need her mother's signature.

When she was thirty-seven Máirín wrote about her experience of living in bedsitters (a one room flat where you shared a bathroom). With some feeling she reflected, "I need to be alone: we all have our own idea of hell and mine is a place where for every moment of my life I would be in company with someone else."[21] The article had the accurate title of 'Bedsitter Bliss'

From a young age Máirín had developed clear views about marriage. 'When I was six I told my mother when I get married I am going to marry a sailor. When asked why, I replied – Because he would be away most of the time.' Some thirty years later her views hadn't changed. In a review of a book about marriage Máirín wrote, "My

---

21 *The Irish Times*, 3rd December 1975

qualifications for reviewing a book about marriage are nil. I am not married. Apart from the odd wish that there was someone at home to feed the cat when I go to prison I have never wanted to be married."[22]

Máirín, as a single woman, always had strong views about how she and other single people should be treated in society. In 1974 then Minister for Local Government James Tully suggested that local authorities might house single people in hostels rather than giving them flats. An angry Máirín responded by declaring that "Single people are not freaks and should not be treated as such by shoving them out of sight into hostels until they redeem themselves by finding a mate. They are valuable members of any community, and they deserve to be considered equally"[23]

Máirín remained true to her beliefs. She never married and she certainly was never shoved out of sight.

Bray Cumann

Máirín joined the local Sinn Féin cumann in Bray where most of the members were in their 40s. There were weekly meetings, and the members sold the party newspaper *The United Irishman*. Apart from Máirín there was one other young member, a youthful and charismatic man named Seamus Costello who was a couple of years older than her. They became friends

---

22 *The Irish Times*, 8th December 1973
23 *The Irish Times*, 3rd October 1974

and went out together a few times.He was Máirín's first boyfriend. (Costello went on to become a hard-line republican figure and Máirín's future colleague Tony Heffernan has speculated whether his idea of a romantic night out was bringing his girlfriend down to the Four Courts to show her the bullet holes in the walls.)[24] Máirín also joined Cumann na mBan, which could be described as a support organisation for the IRA.

Sinn Féin cumann members in Bray, c.1958.
Máirín is second from left. De Burca archive.

While Máirín was pleased to be finally active in Sinn Féin, the party in 1954 could not be described as a political powerhouse. And, of course, when you joined Sinn Féin you became 'inextricably linked', to use a well-worn phrase, with its sister organisation, the IRA. Party historian Brian

24 Tony Heffernan interview.

Feeney is clear in his assessment that "Throughout the years 1950 to 1962 Sinn Féin's Árd Comhairle (the ruling body) was dominated by the IRA".[25] In other words, there may have been two organisations but there was only one boss.

In the post second world war years Sinn Féin began to recover from the restrictions of the war, which included internment for some members. Fianna Fáil was in government and nationalism began to reassert itself. So too did the IRA. From the early 1950s its leadership began to acquire weapons for a military campaign against the British in Northern Ireland.

In this environment those involved on the political side were regarded by the IRA with suspicion. Sinn Féin was an abstentionist party which meant in the South that it would not take Dáil seats in what was regarded as an 'illegitimate state'. And there was certainly no appetite for anything that smacked of radical or left-wing politics. Even at her young age Máirín considered the party to be very right wing.

Border Campaign

The IRA launched a military campaign in Northern Ireland in December 1956 with an attack on bridges, a BBC transmitter and military buildings. Eighteen-year-old Seamus Costello led a unit which destroyed a

---

25   Brian Feeney – *Sinn Féin: A Hundred Turbulent Years*, Ch.6 (O'Brien Press, 2002)

courthouse in Magherafelt, County Derry.[26] They called it Operation Harvest but it subsequently became known as the Border Campaign.

Sinn Féin in its statement of support said they "are proud of the risen nation and appeal to the people of Ireland to assist in every way they can the soldiers of the Irish Republican Army."[27] Sean Garland, who was to figure prominently in Máirín's later career, led an attack on RUC barracks in Brookeborough, County Fermanagh and, after being badly wounded, he was fortunate to escape across the Border.[28]

Máirín thought the whole idea of the campaign was wonderful. "In those years we were like the Provos. It was Brits out and all would be well if the Brits left. Totally ignoring the Unionist population."[29] The reality of the campaign was very different. Máirín's future colleague in Sinn Féin, Michael Ryan, was a leading participant and recounts the whole futile experience in his memoir.

Ryan joined the IRA in 1954 when he was eighteen. Two years later, with limited training, he headed North. He recalls that "We were imbued with an almost fanatical belief in the righteousness of our cause and our methods,

---

26 ibid
27 Ibid
28 Brian Hanley and Scott Miller – *The Lost Revolution: The story of the Official IRA and the Workers Party*, ch.1 (Penguin Ireland, 2009)
29 Irish Times Women's Podcast

and believed the people of Ireland couldn't but support us. We were convinced that we were the true inheritors of the republican tradition and followers of the men of 1916."[30]

With what turned out to be blind optimism Ryan and his colleague talked of the opening phase of the campaign lasting a few months with a couple of them suggesting that they would have the conflict 'won' by March 1957, just three months later. They were to be bitterly disappointed.

Comedy of Errors

Nothing was achieved during the campaign and if it wasn't so serious, the whole affair could be described as a comedy of errors. Operations were littered with ill equipped and poorly dressed 'volunteers' tramping around the mountains of Armagh and spending their nights shivering in damp dug outs. There was gelignite that didn't explode and on one occasion a bomb went off prematurely killing some volunteers.[31]

With great anticipation rockets and bazookas were smuggled in from America but they turned out to be duds. One year into the campaign the government introduced internment in July 1957 and many IRA men were sent to

---

30 Michael Ryan – *My Life in the IRA: The Border Campaign*, Afterword (Mercier Press, 2018)

31 op. cit., ch 4

the prison camp in the Curragh, County Kildare. Ryan estimates that at that point some 95% of the volunteers were in jail.[32] It was not surprising that Ryan himself was caught in 1958 and interned in the Curragh for twelve months.[33]

One of the others to be interned at that time was future TD, MEP and government minister, Proinsias De Rossa. As a twelve-year-old boy he had joined Na Fianna, which was a republican version of the boy scouts, with a little bit of Irish history and republican analysis thrown in. When De Rossa was sixteen he was invited to join the IRA but had no involvement in the Border Campaign.

One Sunday afternoon in 1957 when thirty-seven members of Na Fianna were hiking in Wicklow, they were surrounded by Gardaí and all thirty seven ended up being arrested. They were sentenced to three months imprisonment, for what they didn't know, and taken to Mountjoy jail in Dublin. As their sentences came to an end they were offered a choice – sign a form saying they accepted the Irish constitution or else be interned. De Rossa, and most of his colleagues, refused to sign and he was interned from July 1957 until January 1959.[34]

The Border campaign limped on and after his release Michael Ryan returned to the front line. 'Successes' were few and far between but when they happened, they were

---

32 Ibid
33 Hanley and Miller, ch. 1
34 Proinisas De Rossa Interview

celebrated. Ryan and his squad managed to blow up an RUC jeep but were disappointed to learn afterwards that while two constables had been seriously injured, no one was killed.[35]

Weapons Training

Back in Bray Máirín was doing her bit to help the cause. And despite her later pacifism she recalls that she "would have shot people in those days, anyone up north that I was asked to shoot."[36] One of her first tasks was to engage in some small arms training. 'Myself and another girl went to a house in Crumlin (on Dublin's south side) belonging to a ferocious republican from Cork. In the sitting room he had a big gun, and I could barely carry it never mind fire it. He said to us – 'You never point a gun at anybody unless you intend to fire it. Now this one isn't loaded' and he then aimed it at the fireplace and the thing went off with a deafening bang. The bullet literally shot past my leg. He said – 'I have to congratulate you ladies, most women would be hysterical'. But I was so shocked I was stunned into silence, and I just sat there deaf. He didn't know there was a bullet in it. That was our last involvement in arms training'.

However, a number of years later Eamonn Farrell, a future colleague of Máirín's in the Dublin Housing Action Committee (DHAC), was surprised to come

---

35 Feeney, op.cit, ch 6
36 Irish Times Women's Podcast

across Máirín at what was euphemistically called a 'training camp' in the Wicklow mountains. "I was surprised to see her and she was surprised to see me… It was weapons training… It was almost done to keep some people happy (as there wasn't any 'activity' at the time). I was a bit shocked. I don't think we said anything to each other."[37]

Máirín and Cumann na mBan colleagues attend the Wolfe Tone commemoration in Bodenstown, the burial site of Wolfe Tone. c. 1957, Máirín is 2nd from right. De Burca archive.

Women, often Cumann na mBan members, were regarded as less likely to be targeted by the guards, so they were often used to carry messages or hide 'stuff'. In Máirín's case the 'stuff' was gelignite which she stored in her bedroom in Bray. 'It was there for months, and it started to smell. A previous colleague had also stored

---

37 Eamonn Farrell interview

'stuff' which exploded and maimed her and this was on my mind. I told one of the lads and he was shocked I still had it, took it off me straight away and dumped it into the Dargle River. It wasn't exciting, it was just what you did if you were part of the movement.'

Máirín had very clear views at that time about the use of physical force. 'They were thinking of letting women join the IRA and I would have joined, no doubt about it.' In Cathal Black's film on her life she recalled that during the Border Campaign she was totally approving of the use of physical force and would have clapped the IRA on the back.[38]

While Máirín couldn't join the IRA her friend and colleague Seamus Costello was a prominent member and at times he called on her for help. 'I was living in a house owned by two elderly ladies and there was a strict 'no men allowed' rule. One night Seamus wanted to have an IRA meeting in our flat. I went out and Seamus came in with about ten men. When I came back one of the landladies was waiting for me. Seamus, who could charm the birds off the trees, told the landlady it was a meeting of the local handball club and she ended up giving him the dining room instead. But I got a warning.

Later on, with the Border Campaign well underway I was asked to wash clothes for the IRA volunteers on the run. One day the landlady looked out the window and saw a

---

38 Cathal Black, film

line of men's shirts and pullovers, that was a bridge too far and we had to go.'

1957 Election

Despite the ongoing failure of the Border Campaign, nationally Sinn Féin experienced a brief resurgence. In the 1957 General Election they put forward nineteen candidates and four were elected, one of them being Ruairí Ó Brádaigh, who went on to become President of Provisional Sinn Féin.

Those elected followed the abstentionist policy and did not take their seats in the Dáil. The party's resurgence was to be short lived as new Taoiseach Eamon De Valera set out to stop the IRA with his introduction of internment without trial. The IRA campaign was severely damaged and in the next election four years later, Sinn Féin lost all their seats.

By 1960, three years into the Border Campaign, proposals to end it were being considered by the IRA but it was decided to carry on. They struggled on for another two years but eventually the decision was made, at a meeting in Máirín's now hometown of Bray, to bring it to an end.

Before it was announced publicly, Ó Brádaigh visited Máirín to explain the decision. 'I had helped Ruari when he was on the run and he wanted to show me the statement so I wouldn't see it in the papers. I was very upset. I felt my dream of reunification was over.'

In its statement, issued in February 1962, the IRA said that "The decision to end the resistance campaign has been taken in view of the general situation. Foremost among the factors motivating this course of action has been the attitude of the general public whose minds have been deliberately distracted from the supreme issue facing the Irish people - the unity and freedom of Ireland."[39] In party historian Brian Feeney's blunt assessment, "The whole exercise had achieved nothing."[40] Michael Ryan's own analysis was equally clear. "I was proud that I had taken part in a campaign for a united Ireland … but we still lost."[41]

After the announcement was made Máirín went home to bed that night and cried herself to sleep. She decided to move on, both from Sinn Féin and from Bray. 'When I resigned from the party it wasn't a wrench. I was out of it for a couple of years. Although I never felt hard done by as a woman - the party President at the time was a woman, Margaret Buckley. I didn't miss the old crowd; the party was very right wing, Éire Nua kind of stuff, very religious and nationalistic.

39 Feeney, op cit, ch.6
40 ibid
41 M. Ryan, op cit, ch. 8

Reflection

After the campaign ended leading figures in the IRA/ Sinn Féin, such as Sean Garland, Cathal Goulding and Tomás MacGiolla, realised that heading up North with guns and a green flag wasn't going to change much. For Máirín, the time away from the party gave her the opportunity to reconsider her view on the use of physical force. The film *Judgement at Nuremburg* had a major impact. "The Nazis believed they were doing the right thing... I think I'm doing the right thing by supporting the gun. I could be as wrong as the Nazis were about this. It got all kind of confused in my mind."[42]

With these thoughts in her head twenty-four-year-old Máirín left Bray and headed for a new job and the bright lights of Dublin. It was 1962 and the capital was to become her home for the next sixty plus years.

---

42 Cathal Black film

4. New Job, Changing Party

Máirín got a job in Dublin as a sales assistant with Ferrier Pollock, a wholesale company, and she worked there for the next seven years. Again, it wasn't particularly exciting work, but it introduced her to the world of trade unionism and soon she was chairperson of the Irish Union of Distributive Workers and Clerks (IUDWC) branch in the company.

Máirín's bosses proved to be very tolerant of her union activities. 'They never bothered me when I went missing for meetings… I think they decided to cut their losses … No one ever asked me where I was going when I went off some afternoons. In 1969 I even went up North for a few days. When I left them to work for Sinn Féin my boss was quite prepared to keep me on.' Ferrier Pollock gave Máirín a reference when she left describing her as being "at all times attentive to her duties … (a woman with) a high degree of intelligence (who) would readily adapt herself to any form of employment."[43]

Union activity was part of Máirín's move to the left, although to her it was also just common sense. 'I was always in the union and joined as soon as I could. Daddy was in a union, and he was very much a union man. My

---

43   Reference from Ferrier Pollock, 1969, De Burca archive

left-wing views developed gradually although I didn't see being in a union as particularly left wing. It was protection for you as a worker. I could never understand why people don't join unions; it's the only protection you have. It's so rational to be in a union, irrational not to.'

Changing Ireland

By the time Máirín had her short break from Sinn Féin in the early 1960s, Ireland was changing and Sinn Féin badly needed to follow suit. What Máirín called the 'Éire Nua, nationalistic stuff' had become outdated and belonged to a different generation. The party's Social and Economic Programme was still based on the papal encyclical *Rerum Novarum* and that had been issued in 1891. In Brian Feeney's assessment "The IRA men who directed Sinn Féin regarded politics as a 'dangerous distraction', and worse still, the route to participation in the State."[44]

Old IRA/Sinn Féin leaders like Pádraig Mac Lógáin and Tony Magan "were rigidly conservative and unbending in every aspect. They would not and could not change."[45] This inability to change came to a tragic end for Mac Lógáin, who at one time was party president. A proposal he made about the relationship between the IRA and Sinn Féin was defeated by the party hierarchy and he resigned in 1962, ending his half a century involvement with the

44 Feeney, ch.6
45 ibid

republican movement. In July 1964 he shot himself in his back garden. Máirín was told that Mac Lógáin left a note to say that Cathal Goulding (IRA chief of staff and one of the radicals in the party) wasn't to be blamed.

Despite this set back the badly needed changes started to happen in Sinn Féin. Tomás MacGiolla, a man with left wing views, became party President in 1962 and combined this with being head of the IRA's army council. Seamus Costello was still active in the IRA and Cathal Goulding was the IRA's Chief of Staff. Billy Mc Millen became the new commander of the IRA in the North and others such as Seán Garland began to reassert themselves. A new Social and Economic Programme was adopted, and Goulding was attempting to turn the IRA toward social issues. Volunteers got involved in agitating on evictions in Cork and housing problems in Dublin. An internal IRA review went so far as to recommend that the abstentionist policy be dropped. This, however, was a bridge too far at the time and it was roundly defeated.[46]

In a sign of its broader focus Sinn Féin decided to affiliate to the Irish Anti-Apartheid Movement in 1964. More significantly for Máirín, in 1964 and 1965 female telephonists were engaged in industrial action in Dublin and somewhat surprisingly the IRA/Sinn Féin issued a statement of support. Sinn Féin was clearly changing and their support for that strike, which really pleased Máirín, encouraged her to reactivate her political life.

---

46   B. Hanley and S. Millar, op.cit., ch.2

'I re-joined and attended an Árd Fheis in Moran's Hotel in Dublin. I think it was 1964 or 1965. Cathal Goulding had come back to Ireland after being released from jail in Britain and was determined to oust the old leadership. I didn't know them as I was just a foot soldier. When the vote for membership of the Árd Comhairle came there was a clean sweep, they were all gone. People like Cathal(Goulding), Tomás (Mac Giolla) and Éamonn Mac Thomáis came in. It needed that injection... I was very fond of Tomás, he was a thinker who didn't just rush into decisions.'

For Máirín, Cathal Goulding was 'very intelligent... he was self-taught and became a socialist... he was very influenced by Mick O'Riordan (leader of the Communist Party of Ireland). I was fond of Cathal and did a lot of work for him.'

General Secretary

The party continued to develop and soon Máirín was to become more centrally involved. In 1965 party secretary Éamonn Mac Thomáis wanted to step aside to concentrate on the following year's events to mark the 50th anniversary of the Easter Rising. Máirín was asked would she run to take his place. 'His proposed successor was very right-wing, and I was asked to run to prevent her being elected. I was a bit reluctant because a few years previously when I was in Bray I was put forward and I only got the few votes from Bray. But Seamus Costello took me aside and said to me 'Máirín, don't be so naïve.' The list had gone out and members were mandated to vote for me. I became party secretary (at that time an unpaid position) in 1965 and also a member of the Árd Comhairle.' While this might have been seen as a breakthrough it was also, as Máirín recalled, "because traditionally that was what women did."[47]

While Sinn Féin was changing slowly some issues, such as abstentionism, continued to be very contentious. At the 1966 Árd Fheis, motions to change the policy were defeated. It was a case of -campaigning against apartheid - Yes, but entering the Dáil - No, or certainly not yet.

Anniversary

The 50th anniversary of the Easter Rising in 1966 gave Sinn Féin an opportunity to display its republican credentials. However, their parade through Dublin's O'Connell Street, addressed by Mac Giolla and MacThomáis, only attracted two hundred and fifty supporters. *The Irish Times* noted that "spectators seemed to consist mainly of people returning home from cinemas or public houses who listened to the speakers for a few moments before catching the last bus home."[48]

Máirín attended a parade in the North to mark the anniversary of the Easter Rising, which was one of her

---

47   Tara Keenan Johnson, *Irish Women and Street Politics 1956-1973* ch.3 (Irish Academic Press, 2010)
48   *The Irish Times*, 18th April 1966

few contacts with her northern colleagues at that time. The IRA was determined to show they were alive and kicking and the government in the South was equally determined to prevent them hijacking the celebrations. Both Cathal Goulding and Seán Garland were arrested during the year. Most spectacularly, Nelson's Pillar in Dublin's O'Connell Street was blown up in March 1966, although the IRA denied responsibility.

Another Sinn Féin/IRA parade through the streets of Dublin in 1966 led to running battles with the guards. Máirín's future colleague, seventeen-year-old Tony Heffernan, attended and had his first encounter with the guards. "I got a couple of whacks of a baton along with anyone else who got in their way. That was my first political outing, and I wrote a letter to Sinn Féin applying to join. They never replied and it took me two years to forgive them for the snub until I applied again."[49]

The leftward course of the party was highlighted when Seamus Costello said in his oration at Bodenstown, the burial place of Wolfe Tone, that "the policy of the movement was that key industries be nationalised … and that the large estates owned by absentee landlords be compulsorily purchased and worked on a cooperative basis."[50] The party leadership now believed that they had to get involved in social and economic issues if they were to remain relevant.

49 Brian. Kenny – *Tony Heffernan: From Merrion Square to Merrion Street*, ch.1 (Brian Kenny/Personal History Publishing 2013)
50 Hanley and Millar, op cit, ch 2

Candidate

At the Sinn Féin Árd Fheis in 1967 Cathal Goulding went as far as proposing an amendment to the party's constitution which would see it supporting a 'democratic socialist republic'.[51] For his part Seamus Costello was continually pushing hard to have the abstentionist policy ended. Máirín was now more prominent in the party, being both Secretary and a member of the Árd Comhairle.

In 1967 twenty-nine-year-old Máirín had her first outing in electoral politics when she was a candidate for Sinn Fein in the local elections. She ran in the inner-city Ushers Quay Ward of Dublin Corporation (now Dublin City Council). Sinn Fein's abstentionist policy did not extend to participation in local government. The election was an eye-opening experience for Máirín who saw when canvassing the appalling housing conditions many people had to endure. It was an important motivating factor in her involvement in housing action campaigns. Máirín got 467 votes but wasn't elected. She did, however, finish ahead of Mick O' Riordan from the Communist Party who got less than 300 votes.

Around this time Máirín also began her long career as a public speaker. At a meeting in Sligo in 1968 she condemned private ownership of rivers and fisheries and said that "Sinn Féin, if given a mandate from the people, would have the strength and ability to take over privately

---

51 op. cit, ch 3

run fisheries and it is now up to the people to strengthen their demand for nationalisation."[52] Strong words but Máirín was also recognising the need for engagement in democratic politics.

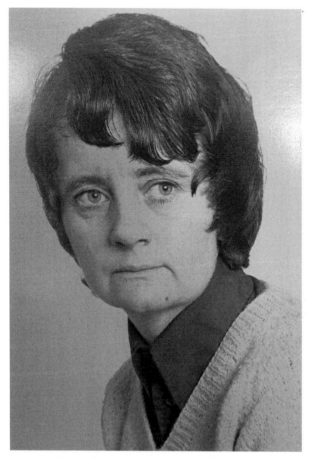

Photo used in Máirín's 1967 local election campaign.
De Burca archive.

Before the end of the decade Máirín moved also from being 'Burke' to 'De Burca'. 'I decided in the1960s to have another try at learning Irish and, as a start, use the

---

52 *Sligo Champion,* 1st November 1968

Irish form of my name. Alas I only achieved one of those ambitions and it is a major disappointment in my life.'

Abstention

At Sinn Fein's 1968 Árd Fheis Tomás Mac Giolla was confident enough to proclaim that if the party won a majority of Dáil seats they would enter the parliament. The following year a commission was established to examine the whole abstention issue and consider if it was still relevant.[53]

Máirín was pro-abstention when she re-joined the party. 'I think it was tradition, would we be letting down the people who went before us if we dropped it? Seamus (Costello) was always pushing to end it. Then I heard Tomás, someone I respected a lot, speak in favour of ending it. That shocked me and forced me to reassess my own position and eventually I backed dropping it.'

As Sinn Féin moved into the momentous years of 1968 and 1969 it had changed dramatically since Máirín re-joined a few years earlier. Tony Heffernan, a teenager at the time, recalled, "there was a real sense…that we were on the verge of a very profound change all over the world. With the arrogance and confidence that only 18 year olds can have, we were sure we were on the verge of revolution."[54]

53 Feeney, ch 7
54 Kenny, ch.2

*Máirín outside the Sinn Féin offices in Gardiner Place, Dublin.
c.1971. De Burca archive*

By 1968 Máirín wasn't an idealistic teenager. She was in her 30th year and firmly established in Sinn Féin. She was strong in her left-wing views and had already taken to the streets in protest. The next decade of her life was to be one of extraordinary radicalism, activism and social struggle.

5. Action On Housing

While Sinn Féin was moving with the times, state housing provision in the 1960s was stuck firmly in the last century, particularly in Dublin. Tenements, overcrowded and unsanitary, were commonplace. The provision of local authority housing, which developed well in the 1940s and 1950s in the city's suburbs, had stalled.

Housing Deaths

Dublin's appalling housing situation came to a head in 1963 when tenement houses collapsed in Fenian Street and Bolton Street, killing four people, two of them young girls. In an effort to avert further tragedy Dublin Corporation evacuated over 150 houses which held over 500 families. Some of these families were moved to Griffith Barracks which provided emergency hostel accommodation.

Conditions in Griffith Barracks were as bad as the tenements and one day the families there decided they had had enough. A young Des Geraghty was walking past the Barracks when he came across "a large, bedraggled band of men, women and children pushing prams, carrying children, trying to hold onto shoes and clothing."[55] Geraghty came from a republican family and had inherited a strong sense of social justice. He talked to two of the protestors, Dennis and Mary Dennehy, who told him they were marching into O'Connell Street in protest against their living conditions, which included husbands and wives being separated.

Geraghty and his friend joined in, took part in the protest and then learned that the families had nowhere to go that night. Geraghty who had been a member of Na Fianna, the 'Republican Boy Scouts', knew that there were large tents in Na Fianna's HQ in nearby Mountjoy Square. The tents were acquired, and the families camped in the Square for a number of days.

Daily protests were held, and Labour politician John O Connell was supportive. As the protests weren't yielding results a more radical plan was hatched. "We were going to occupy Nelson's Pillar, lock ourselves in with supplies and hang a big banner from the top highlighting the homeless problem. However, when John O'Connell heard about this he got very upset and thought the IRA was taking over. He got some well-off people to put up money and bought mobile homes for the families."[56]

The families scattered and the sting was taken out of this particular protest but there was much more to come in the next few years. Máirín, now with a more developed sense

---

55 Des Geraghty – *We Dare To Dream Of An Island Of Equal* , ch.14 (Red Stripe Press, 2021)
56   Des Geraghty interview

of social justice and in her capacity as Sinn Féin party secretary, got involved in the Mountjoy Square protest and this was where Geraghty and herself crossed paths for the first time. There were many more protests to come for them both and as Geraghty recalls, "Every campaign after that she would be there and every courageous move she would lead. Máirín was the Joan of Arc of the working class."[57]

Housing Action Committee

Proinsias De Rossa had left his Na Fianna days long behind him and was now focused on social and political activity. He had read about Citizen Advice Bureaux (CAB) in England and how people on the left in Britain organised. With the support of Sinn Féin's North Dublin City cumann he set up a CAB in Dublin's Mountjoy Square and virtually everyone who came in the door had a housing problem. De Rossa's next move was to organise people to campaign on the issue and Máirín was one of the first people to sign up. Another Sinn Féin activist, Sean O'Cionnaith, who had been involved in the housing action group Shelter in Britain got involved as well.[58]

Máirín had already some experience of knocking on doors for Sinn Féin during her local election campaign in 1967. 'It was an education. Housing was a major, major problem and conditions in the private rented sector were

---

57 ibid
58 Proinsias De Rossa interview

appalling.' In Dublin's inner city some flats in Benburb Street had one cold tap for each house and one outside toilet. The need for action was apparent.

These various activists quickly came together and in May 1967 formed the Dublin Housing Action Committee (DHAC). On the Sinn Féin side key figures were De Rossa, O'Cionnaith and Máirín. The other leading figures who were themselves homeless included Denis and Mary Dennehy, Paddy Stanley and Bernard Browne. They were joined later by others, such as Eamonn Farrell.

By the following year the DHAC had managed to engage 'members' from the Communist Party, the Labour Party, Sinn Féin, Maoists, Trotskyites, members of the Salvation Army, members of the St. Vincent De Paul, various students, some Catholic clergy and eccentric heiress Hilary Boyle.[59] Máirín described it in a similar manner when she recalled that "There was the Housing Action Committee, the Irish Voice on Vietnam, the Anti-Apartheid Movement and Irish Women's Liberation Movement. One led to another; they all became part of the whole."[60]

In left wing circles, this large coalition of interests was nothing short of miraculous. Inevitably, however, there were disagreements. 'There would be arguments into the night regarding what slogan would be put on the

---

59 Tara Keenan Thomson -*Irish Women and Street Politics 1956-1973*, Ch. 3 (Irish Academic Press, 2010)

60 Ibid

placards. For one event the Maoists arrived with a large banner of Chairman Mao and copies of his Little Red Book. They weren't allowed join the march and ended up walking on the footpath.'

DHAC had five key demands which included the declaration of a housing emergency, a prohibition on the demolition of sound houses, repair of dwellings when landlords refused to renovate them and an end to the building of office blocks. In a 1968 interview Máirín declared that "It is necessary for us to be agitators, but the government misconstrues our objectives. We agitate solely for the implementation of our five-point plan."[61]

City Hall

The first DHAC protest was outside Dublin Corporation's (now Dublin City Council) City Hall. Máirín later recalled, "My colleagues and I gave the masses a full half hour to turn up and when they didn't, we started off anyway, six of us, including two carrying our rather impressive banner. We tried to make our demonstration look more formidable by marching in twos, but there were still only three rows."[62]

A short time later, at another protest, their numbers were reduced further. 'There were about five of us and we were walking up and down with our placards and after

---

61   *The Irish Times,* 17th June 1968
62   *The Irish Times,* 21st December 1979

about fifteen minutes this priest arrived, took up one of the placards and joined the picket. We were gobsmacked and thought he must have joined the wrong protest. One of our members, Hilary Boyle, had a posh accent so we got her to talk to him. He explained that he was a Jesuit priest and had been promised a flat in Ballymun by the Corporation. His name was Fr. Michael Sweetman. and he came to a lot of our meetings and spoke on our platform. He was a lovely man.'

Sweetman's involvement gave the new organisation a level of respectability they would have struggled otherwise to attain. However, then Minister for Finance Charlie Haughey described him in the Dáil as "a gullible priest who didn't know anything about anything."[63]

Marches took place and public meetings were organised in Dublin's O'Connell Street. Alongside the pickets outside City Hall, DHAC members would go into the public gallery at the Corporation's monthly meetings and heckle the city councillors. On one occasion Mary Dennehy threw a rat from the public gallery into the chamber.[64] This action was condemned by Sean Dunne, the Lord Mayor, but Máirín was having none of it. In a letter to *The Irish Press* she wrote that Mrs. Dennehy "who introduced (the Lord Mayor) to the rodent, lives in a caravan, has no running water or toilets and has

---

63 Dáil Debates, 2nd May 1968
64 Des Geraghty interview

three children."[65] In other words, until we see action the protests will continue.

De Rossa's colleague Sean O Cionnaith had a great capacity to get publicity and the activities of the DHAC were reported regularly in the media. The State's main response to the crisis was to commission the Ballymun tower blocks in the mid-1960s, with each of the towers named after one of the leaders of the 1916 rising. Ballymun was a huge undertaking but clearly could not meet the immediate needs of all of Dublin's homeless.

Attacks

The protests outside City Hall were regular events and inevitably involved Máirín and her colleagues appearing in the District Court. In July 1968 they were charged with a breach of the peace by using a loudspeaker outside the Hall when a meeting was taking place. In Court Máirín denied that she was an agitator but did own up to being a revolutionary. She accused the guards of police brutality and claimed that "the police have been attacking us for forty years."[66] Given that Máirín was aged thirty at the time that might have been something of an exaggeration.

From the beginning, the issue of 'overzealous' guards was a serious concern. In May 1968 an *Irish Times* editorial opened with a surprising sentence. "When the Students'

---

65 *The Irish Press*, no date
66 *The Irish Times*, 23rd July 1968

Representative Council of Trinity College takes it upon itself to send an official complaint to the Minister for Justice specifying brutality by the Gardai, the allegation deserves close examination."[67]

Eamonn Farrell, DHAC secretary, being arrested by nine guards, after a housing protest in College Green, Dublin in 1969. Photo: Courtesy of Rolling News.

The editorial went on to detail how reporters saw a lady "who is conspicuous in these occasions (probably Mary Dennehy) hit a Garda detective in the face with her umbrella …. one of these reporters saw a guard hit a girl on the head and shoulders (with a baton) and again when she was on the ground."[68] In effect, it was hand to hand combat.

In conclusion *The Irish Times* wrote, "there are too many

---

67 *The Irish Times*, 14th May 1968
68 ibid

accounts by reliable witnesses of acts of unnecessary roughness and sometimes brutality by individual guards to make the most recent complaints seem frivolous."[69] The issue of Garda brutality was to be a constant feature throughout the many protests and occupations held by the DHAC and indeed throughout Máirín's later campaigning life.

Crisis Magazine

In the spirit of the 1960s the DHAC was a radical, direct action organisation. In the first issue of its magazine, *Crisis*, the group stated that its aim was "to organise all the homeless people in Dublin into a mass militant body to agitate against the appalling housing situation that now exists."[70] They called on all homeless families to join the DHAC and to occupy all vacant private accommodation.

In the same magazine the organisation detailed the appalling treatment of families by private landlords, with the landlords being named and shamed. In a nice Jesuitical turn of phrase Fr Sweetman, referring to some activities of Dennis Dennehy, wrote that what he did was, strictly speaking, illegal but it was not immoral.[71]

---

69   ibid
70   Dublin Housing Action Committee – *Crisis: Bulletin No 1* (no date)
71   ibid

March April

Bulletin No 1

CRISIS

DUBLIN HOUSING ACTION COMMITTEE   SIXPENCE

Front cover of the 1st issue of the DHAC's magazine, Crisis.
c. 1967. De Burca archive

One of DHAC's first challenges was to make itself known. Máirín recalls, 'We were starting from scratch, and we had to get the public onside. To do that we had to convince them that there was a real problem... a crisis. The first thing we did was sit down in the middle of O'Connell Street at 8 pm every night for a week. Students from University College Dublin (UCD) joined and swelled our ranks. There was mayhem, but it started people asking why we were doing it and we began to get people onside. Many would have known someone living in poor housing. Labour said there was no emergency ... but they had to eat their words.'

Inevitably, some of the publicity was negative and there were scare headlines in some newspapers about 'Reds and Communists'. Fr. Michael Cleary, then a catholic parish curate, claimed that Sinn Féin and the Citizens Advice Bureau were led by communists. Cleary also described the DHAC as 'wreckers who hold up traffic'. His claims were strongly refuted by Sinn Féin President, Tomás MacGiolla, who challenged him to produce evidence to support his claim. None was forthcoming.[72] Fr. Cleary went on to become a well known personality on TV and radio and developed a career as 'The Singing Priest'. While a priest Cleary had two children with his housekeeper. That aspect of his life was less well publicised.

Dennis Dennehy

The situation of one of DHAC's leading members, Dennis Dennehy and his family, led to high profile protests and occupations. Dennehy and his wife were a formidable couple. At one protest Mary Dennehy started hitting a Garda superintendent with an umbrella with husband Dennis wading in to lend support. The Dennehys were regular attenders at all the protests and often called on trade union activist, Rosheen Callender, and her friend to babysit. However, on one occasion the Dennehys went

---

72 *The Irish Times,* 6th December 1968

off on a demonstration and then disappeared for the weekend, leaving the child minders literally holding the baby.[73] That might be described as taking liberties in the cause of justice.

The Dennehys had been living in a John O'Connell bought caravan and in 1968 they squatted in a house in Mountjoy Square. The landlord refused their offer to pay rent and got a court injunction to evict them. The Dennehys refused to comply and in January 1969 Denis Dennehy ended up in Mountjoy jail where he commenced a hunger strike.

DHAC protest in Dublin's O'Connell St. at the jailing of Dennis Dennehy. 1969. Courtesy National Photographic Archive and Independent newspaper archive.

73 Rosheen Callender interview

The timing of Dennehy's hunger strike was hardly accidental. This was January 1969 and Dennehy and the DHAC knew that the 50th anniversary of the 1st Dáil was coming up that month. There were large scale protests and concern expressed at the family's situation. Frank Cluskey, then Dublin's Lord Mayor, sent a telegram to Taoiseach, Jack Lynch, appealing for Dennehy's release. The *Irish Independent* claimed that "What happened to Denis Dennehy on the eve of the first Dáil's 50th anniversary must never be allowed happen again. The gaoling of homeless Denis Dennehy should be the last indignity we allow the homeless to suffer."[74] It was strong stuff from a hardly radical newspaper, but Jack Lynch and every other politician would not interfere in a court decision.

Confronting Dev

On the day of the Dáil anniversary, 1916 veteran Joe Clarke interrupted an event in the Mansion House by calling for Dennehy's release. And needless to say, Máirín De Burca wanted to play her part in embarrassing the government. 'We decided to occupy the Custom House, but I was late and got lost. I could hear other people being arrested. My colleague and I went and sat outside a door and then someone brought us in, and we had a long discussion about housing. We didn't like to say – don't be doing this, we want to be arrested.'

---

74 *Irish Independent*, 21st January, 1969

'We then decided to head back to the Sinn Féin office and as we passed the Pro-Cathedral, we saw De Valera's (the President's) car. Without breaking stride, I swerved past a guard and inside. They sent in a guard who stupidly stood in front of me. I waited until the mass was over and Dev came down the aisle. I didn't want to give him a heart attack. I kept my distance, came out from behind the guard and shouted –'release Denis Dennehy and house the homeless.' I finally got myself arrested.'

The Irish Independent reported on Máirín's arrest in a displeased manner. "A woman, who shouted abusively in the Pro-Cathedral as dignitaries were leaving after the commemorative mass… was removed by a uniformed Garda and bundled into a squad car. President De Valera was leading the distinguished attendance from the church when the woman moved forward from the body of the worshippers and shouted, 'Release Dennis Dennehy.' The procession paused for a few minutes while she was hurriedly taken outside."[75]

Máirín and a number of others were charged with violent and riotous behaviour and using insulting words. Somewhat surprisingly, the judge held that the evidence did not show that Máirín's behaviour was violent, riotous or insulting and he dismissed both charges.[76] It was one up for the Irish legal system, which established you could shout at the President after mass and get away with it.

---

75 *The Irish Independent*, 22nd January 1969
76 *Irish Examiner*, 12th February 1969

All of the protests did have an impact and a way was found to release Dennehy from jail. This affair, if nothing else, gave huge publicity to DHAC and the homeless problem in the city. Unfortunately, there were no quick solutions and the protests continued.

In September 1969 five members of the DHAC went even further. They found their way into the Four Courts building, barricaded themselves into one of the courts and put up a sign which said 'DHAC: We are occupying the Four Courts to demand the release of jailed homeless'. They were referring to two squatters who were sent to prison after refusing to leave a vacant hotel in Dublin's Harcourt Street.

A large number of Gardaí arrived, broke down the barricade and, according to Eric Fleming, one of the protestors, "kicked us and beat us all over the room." Fleming said he was forced to sit on the floor and was beaten with the leg of a chair. A young girl, Isolda Byrne, said she was kicked in the head, mouth and body and a Garda told her to "Get up you bitch" and kicked her again.[77] She ended up with a cut lip and bruises on her face. Given all this happened within the Four Courts it could be described as very rough justice.

O'Connell Bridge Battle

The challenge for DHAC was to come up with different ways of keeping the housing crisis in the public's mind,

---

77 *The Irish Times,* 26th September 1969

in the newspapers and on television. O'Connell Street, Dublin's main thoroughfare, was often chosen for protests. Stopping the traffic and holding up the city was always going to get attention.

Encounters with the guards on O' Connell Street and its bridge were regular occurrences. One large protest attracted thousands of supporters and when they stopped and took over the bridge the guards seemed totally unprepared and resorted to force. Des Geraghty was in the middle of it. "When we sat down the batons came out straight away. I saw Máirín being batoned and we went to her assistance and then we were batoned… the police waded in. We were resisting them and fighting back. One of my friends fell and the police started kicking him. I screamed 'You killed him, you killed him.' At which the guard ran off. My friend then 'recovered' and ran off with the same guard giving chase. We all then ran and took shelter in *The Irish Times* offices on D'Olier Street."[78]

A number of the protestors were then arrested and taken to nearby Pearse Street Garda station. A crowd gathered outside chanting 'release the prisoners, release the prisoners'. Unfortunately for Geraghty, his friend had been arrested and his mother arrived to berate Geraghty for leading her son astray. As she dramatically put it 'If his father was alive today, he'd be turning in his grave'.

Help arrived in the form of two 'professional' type women, Mrs Margaret Gaj, who owned Dublin's

78 Des Geraghty interview

'bohemian restaurant', and Dr Moira Woods, both of whom went on to be key activists in the Women's Liberation Movement. Woods insisted on seeing the Inspector in charge and promptly marched into the station and down to the cells to check on the prisoners and to conduct a head count. The protestors stayed chanting through the night until eventually the prisoners were released. Apart from a bruised body, one of the end results for Geraghty was considerable difficulty getting a visa to visit his American wife's family.

Squatting Policy

An obvious focus of attention was the Fianna Fail government. Kevin Boland was the Minister for Local Government at the time and in charge of housing provision. Not surprisingly, he became a target. 'Boland lived up the side of a mountain. He was very anti us and quite hard line. We picketed his house, and we were all arrested. They let us out at 3 am and we were in the middle of nowhere. Luckily Sean O Cionnaith managed to phone someone who arranged a relay of cars to get us home.' Boland went on to denounce the DHAC as the creation of an illegal organisation.

The policy of DHAC was to squat homeless families only in private properties. They discouraged people from squatting in Dublin Corporation houses or flats while at the same time supporting families who faced eviction. In a defence of their approach, Máirín as the group's

PRO wrote in a letter to *Hibernia* magazine (which she went on to work for) that the group had squatted twenty families in private property and had also prevented or reversed thirty evictions from both public and private dwellings. She suggested that "If the DHAC had been responsible for 500 private property squatters we would be more than proud and happy to say so... We have never refused a call for help from a family being evicted and we make no apology to anyone for this activity."[79]

This policy inevitably led to a series of confrontations with the guards and the criminal justice system. How these various 'battles' played out illustrates the types of protest that were commonplace in the 1960s and 1970s. It shows also how the State's sometimes ruthless response to any radical public dissent was influenced by events which were unfolding at the same time in the North of Ireland.

Sara Place was a small group of run down cottages in the suburb of Inchicore which the authorities were keen to demolish, planning to move the residents to other locations. 'One of our first battles was over this small group of tiny cottages. They were moving people out, but the alternatives weren't suitable. We protested and I remember we had a mole in Dublin Corporation who told us when they were coming to evict the families. I saw the guards assembling and taking off their coats. It looked like they were preparing for battle.'

---

79 *Hibernia,* 2nd-16th April 1971

'I was scared but Mick O' Riordan, from the Communist Party, came along and showed the workers his union card and that paused the eviction. That was my first serious arrest, and we were charged with breaching the peace.' Máirín's Sinn Fein colleague Michael Ryan avoided being charged when he escaped from the Garda van as it was driving into the Bridewell police station.[80] The group's solicitor Con Lehane managed to get them off on a technicality. While the families in Sara Place eventually had to move, the pause in proceedings allowed time for proper alternatives to be put in place.

During the 1960s Dublin was ripe for office block development. Old, sometimes Georgian houses, were being bought and left vacant until they were ready for demolition. When the DHAC started its campaign of squatting the homeless, it occupied fairly derelict properties such as in Mountjoy Square, on Dublin's northside. Later they moved upmarket and occupied good properties on streets such as Mount Street, Waterloo Road and Pembroke Road in the well-off suburbs of Dublin's southside.[81]

Students also occupied Georgian houses in Dublin's Hume Street which were planned for redevelopment, and this attracted widespread publicity. But Máirín made clear that she wasn't interested "in having Hume Street preserved as 'a Georgian museum', she was only concerned with the fact that there were 10,000 homeless

80   Hanley and Millar, ch. 3
81   Eamonn Farrell interview

people in Dublin and that these buildings could be preserved in order to house them."[82]

Not all the protests got the same attention as Hume Street. One bank holiday weekend DHAC occupied a property in Mount Street and embarked on a weekend hunger strike as well. There were six protestors, but they attracted no attention. During the weekend Proinsias De Rossa entered one of the rooms to see Communist Party leader Michael O' Riordan eating a sandwich. De Rossa queried this only to be bluntly told 'Who the fuck gives a shit whether I eat a sandwich or not'.[83] Other protests were much more successful.

The Battle of Pembroke Road

The scandal of perfectly good houses being left vacant while their owners planned their 'redevelopment', was always a focus for the campaign. Máirín, as the group's PRO, was particularly trenchant in her criticism. In May 1970 she issued a statement condemning the practice where good houses are "wantonly destroyed to make room for office blocks, for big business and in the process, what used to be one of the finest cities in the world… has been given the appearance of a heavily bombed area being rebuilt by tasteless morons."[84]

---

82 *The Irish Times*, 17th December 1969
83 Proinsias De Rossa interview
84 *DHAC Press Statement,* 26th May 1970. De Burca archive

Eamonn Farrell, who had been living in England and was now back in Ireland and homeless, became one of DHAC's key activists. Farrell took over as secretary from Denis Dennehy. It was a new role for him and Máirín, a previous secretary and not always the most diplomatic, pointed out that he didn't have to make a verbatim record of each meeting and then spend much of the next meeting reading his lengthy minutes.[85]

Farrell and a number of other homeless families proceeded to occupy two adjacent houses on Pembroke Road, in what is now Dublin 4. These were fine properties with one of them owned by the Gallagher building and development company. Apart from housing homeless people, DHAC wanted to highlight the fact that these houses were being deliberately left to deteriorate so they would become uninhabitable and could then be demolished or turned into office accommodation.

The families, despite various attempts to move them out, lived in Pembroke Road for at least a year. The ensuing struggle between owners, squatters, henchmen, the Gardaí and the courts was to become one of the fiercest confrontations of the whole housing action campaign. The story of that battle is worth telling in some detail, both to highlight the overreaction of the guards and the ferocious way in which the squatters fought back. It is also a telling commentary on the State's attitude to protest during those turbulent years.

---

85 Eamonn Farrell interview

Various attempts to rattle the family were made by a brash, young Patrick Gallagher, son of the company's founder, and his friend who would arrive up in Gallagher's sports car, kick the door and shout 'we'll get you out', before running off again. This happened on a regular basis and the squatters decided to get revenge. Working on the basis of using what you have to hand, various receptacles were filled with urine and when Gallagher and his friend came back again, they were absolutely destroyed. It was as rough and basic as that.

Gallagher took over the family business at a young age and was one of the people who funded Charlie Haughey's extravagant lifestyle. However, ten years later *The Sunday Tribune* was reporting that Gallagher, then only 30 years old, was "watching a radically altered business crumble before his eyes."[86] He also served a jail term in the North for financial irregularities and died in his 50s.

Garda Attack

Events took a nastier turn on Pembroke Road when a gang of 'security' men turned up one day, broke down the door of one of the houses and proceeded to evict everything and everybody. It was at a time when all the male occupants were out and when Eamonn Farrell returned he found women and children crying on the doorsteps surrounded by beds, bedclothes and cooking utensils.

---

86 *The Sunday Tribune*, 2nd May 1982

In the heat of the moment Farrell did something "I probably shouldn't have done" and fetched an old, out of action World War One pistol. He went to the house, produced the pistol and said to the security staff – 'We are taking back the house'. With that the security men ran out the back door shouting – 'He has a gun, he has a gun.'"[87]

The house was retaken but Farrell and the other squatters knew there would be a huge reaction. Somehow Máirín was contacted and she arrived promptly on her trusty scooter to spirit the pistol away. Reinforcements arrived to occupy the house and they awaited the inevitable response.

Máirín had been tipped off by a newspaper reporter that a large force of guards was assembling at Donnybrook Garda station and would soon be on its way. 'I went to the window and coming down the road I saw vans, motorcycles, guards with shields... the Inspector came to the front window and I said two or three of you can come in. They said alright but they had already sent men round the back. Suddenly a massive boulder came in the window. Myself and a few others were taken to hospital.'

The Irish Times reported that the house was "raided by a large force of Gardaí and detectives... In ensuing violence at least 12 people were injured and, according to Gardaí, bottles, boiling water, stones and other missiles were

---

87 Eamonn Farrell interview

used against the police." The paper's report continued with one member of the DHAC describing how he saw "Máirín De Burca coming out covered in blood… and that when the Gardai got in they 'just began kicking people around the place.'"[88] Twelve of the squatters were arrested and Máirín, the only woman, was, of course, one of them. And while all this was taking place, Eamonn Farrell, the man with the gun, was sitting uninterrupted in the other occupied house next door.

Court Case

However, Farrell was eventually tracked down and, along with a number of the squatters, he was charged with conspiracy and assaulting the guards. Fortunately for them, due to Máirín's quick response, the pistol issue had literally disappeared. When the case came to court the twelve accused were surprised to see a large media presence and assumed it was for them.

As they entered the District Court, they saw two men in suits waiting for their case to be called, which turned out to be part of the 1970 Arms Trial, where a government minister and three others were accused of illegally smuggling arms into Ireland at the height of the Northern Ireland conflict. The men waiting were future Taoiseach Charles Haughey, one of the accused, and his supporter Neil Blayney.

---

88 *The Irish Times,* 20th May 1970

Not surprisingly, the media had disappeared by the time the squatters' case was called. After all that drama and violence, the charges against all of the accused were dropped when the State didn't put forward any evidence. It seemed to be a strange decision and it is possible that the State did not want the behaviour of the guards to come under scrutiny. Some of those evicted were taken in by the redoubtable Mrs. Gaj and Moira Woods, who was actually legally living in her own house in Ballsbridge.

The DHAC was not to be easily put off by that appearance in court. It called for an enquiry into the whole affair and soon after it proceeded to reoccupy the houses on Pembroke Road. The guards then went to the High Court to get the necessary eviction order. The judge was told the guards might have to call in the military to help with getting the squatters out. To which the judge responded by stating that if the court order could not be executed "we have reached a state of anarchy."[89]

Steel Helmeted Guards

Two months after the initial battle and with their eviction order to hand the guards swooped again, this time with a force of "200 steel helmeted Gardaí." In dramatic fashion *The Irish Press* reported that their dawn raid "was carefully planned and carried through with military precision... Swiftly and silently the first tender load of police moved down the alleyway with ladders

---

89 *The Irish Press,* 1ˢᵗ Jul 1970

and steel bars." It was like something from a thriller movie and the breathless report continued by describing how the guards positioned men on the rooftop and then "several tender loads of helmeted Gardai arrived, armed with batons, iron bars and carrying shields."

The guards were subjected to a barrage of missiles which included bottles, cement, stones and, allegedly, tear gas. Using their shields as protection the guards managed to break through the front door using a chainsaw and soon after a white flag was raised at one of the upstairs windows and ten occupants came out.[90] This time Eamonn Farrell was arrested. And anarchy was averted, at least for a while.

The 'Pembroke Road 10' (nine men and Máirín) were brought in front of the High Court the next day and the number of guards reported to be involved had been reduced to 131, although it included 24 sergeants, 20 inspectors, 4 Superintendents and 1 Chief Superintendent. The phrase a hammer to crack a nut comes to mind.

The Court was told by their legal team that the accused wished to apologise and give undertakings that they would not occupy the Pembroke Road house again. On foot of this Justice Teevan, who had granted the eviction order and was concerned about anarchy in their midst, somewhat surprisingly gave a three-month suspended sentence to all ten squatters. He warned the 'Pembroke

---

90 *The Irish Press*, 3rd September 1970

Road 10' there would be more serious penalties if they interfered with any other properties owned by the Gallagher companies.

As part of his judgement Justice Teevan commented on the protestors refusal to obey a High Court order. "Such a state of affairs would be ruinous to society. It would be the first step to the complete erosion of freedom of citizens."[91] However, how a force of over one hundred guards might need the help of the army to evict ten squatters was not explained.

After the event the Minister for Justice, Des O'Malley weighed in and claimed that "the first time CS gas was used in the twenty six counties was against the police when they were enforcing a civil order from the High Court in Pembroke road."[92] Máirín's future IWLM colleague, Moira Woods, responded with a letter to *The Irish Times* where she pointed out that in the court proceedings which followed, "No one – not even the prosecution witnesses, the Gardai - claimed that CS gas had been used by the squatters or the Housing Action Committee. The gas story is just gas."[93] On this issue it was game, set and match to Dr. Woods.

The huge reaction on behalf of the guards, the government and the courts can only be fully understood by looking at events in the North and to a lesser extent

---

91   *Irish Independent,* 2nd July 1970
92   *The Irish Times,* 11th August 1970
93   *The Irish Times,* 11th August 1970

in the South during 1970. The Troubles were underway, the Provisional IRA had been born and there was a fear, whether understandable or not, that 'subversives' and 'agitators' were threatening the State. Swift and severe action was seen as essential by the authorities.

The 'Battle of Pembroke Road' ended with 'anarchy' avoided and democracy preserved. And, in an interesting footnote, Eamonn Farrell ended up being allocated a flat in the new Ballymun development where he lived for a number of years.

Juries Act

The reaction of the Fianna Fail government to all these protests was unsympathetic and oppressive. In direct response to the DHAC occupations in Pembroke Road and elsewhere they introduced the Prohibition of Forcible Entry and Occupation Bill. When enacted it was more commonly known as the Forcible Entry Act.

By the summer of 1971 the Bill was about to be passed and Máirín and colleagues were protesting outside the Dáil. They tried to lock the gates to prevent the TDs from leaving. Máirín was arrested along with her journalist friend Mary Anderson and they were charged with a breach of the peace. What happened next was to lead to a fundamental change in the operation of the Irish legal system.

In 1971 juries were effectively all male, and property-owning men at that. Women could apply to sit on juries, and many did, but up until Máirín and Mary Anderson's challenge just two women had actually been allowed into a jury box. A Committee on Court Procedure and Practice had recommended in 1962 that women should be able to sit on juries, but this group had some members who disagreed. These dissenters wrote that "If a married woman returns to her home at seven o'clock in the evening and finds an irate husband and three hungry children waiting for her, we think it unlikely that they will accept the importance of jury service as a convincing excuse."[94]

Máirín was ready to act. 'My solicitor Dudley Potter, a lovely man, worked with me for nothing. He suggested we go for a trial by jury which I didn't understand as the jury would be all property-owning men. I approached Mary Robinson, then a young barrister, and she said there's only one way to go – challenge the constitutionality of the Juries Act. She knew we didn't have any money but herself, Donal Barrington (senior counsel and later a Supreme Court judge) and Dudley all worked for nothing.'

Máirín and Mary Anderson sued the Attorney General and in court they claimed the Juries Act was inconsistent with Article 40 of the Constitution which guaranteed equality before the law for all citizens. Their counsel

---

94 *Irish Independent*, 4th May 1971 quoted in Stopper, ch.2

pointed out that "a man with no property who never did a day's work in his life was eligible to serve on a jury if he was lucky enough to marry a rich woman, but there was no corresponding provision in the case of a woman."[95]

It seemed like a convincing case, but it was fought by the State and after years of legal action, and defeat in the High Court, the case ended up in the Supreme Court where in 1975 the Juries Act was found to be unconstitutional. The discrimination against women and people with no property was removed in the 1976 Juries Act.

In his judgement Justice Walsh asked "Can it seriously be suggested that a person who is not the rated occupier… is less intelligent or less honest or less impartial than one who is so rated? The answer could only be in the negative." He went on to declare that "the provision made in the Juries Act was undisguisedly discriminatory on the ground of sex only."[96]

Máirín was obviously pleased with the outcome. 'We were very lucky with the Supreme Court judges we had, people like Brian Walsh who was very liberal. And I remember well the day after the judgement I was back in the Sinn Féin office and this woman rang me, crying and screaming, demanding to know how dare I think she was going to serve on a jury.' The icing on the cake was that the original case against the two women was quietly dropped.

---

95   *Irish Independent*, 30th March 1973
96   *The Irish Times,* 13th December 1975

Máirín and Mary Anderson had achieved something of real significance on behalf of women's equality. Newspaper headlines highlighted the 'victory for women' angle. but there was less emphasis on the equally important removal of the property qualification. After the judgement was issued Máirín and Mary Anderson issued a statement about the 'uninformed comment' about the ruling. They criticised "The frivolous emphasis by the media on the qualification concerning women (which) neatly slides over the more important issue in this case – the abolition of the property clause."[97] It was a hugely important victory, fought by two tenacious women. There were to be many more such battles.

Benburb Street

Being in and out of court over the Juries Act did not get in the way of Máirín and the DHAC's ongoing campaign for better housing. And nor were they going to let the Forcible Entry Act stop them.

Flats in Benburb street were among the worst in the city and it was a place that stayed in Máirín's mind since she had canvassed there in 1967. In 1971 she led a group of about eighty people from the flats into a protest/occupation of the Custom House, the HQ of the Department of Local Government which was then responsible for housing provision. The protestors sang 'We shall not be moved' and demanded the flats be

---

97 Máirín De Burca, Mary Anderson- Press Statement, 14th December 1975, Máirín De Burca Papers/Kings inn

knocked down and vacant buildings be acquired to house the residents. One of the residents told *The Irish Times* they had no light, no electricity and one toilet for ten to twelve people.[98] After a long battle the families were relocated.

Despite the awfulness of the situations, families found themselves in, some protests had a humourous side. On one occasion Máirín sat with a woman and her young children who were about to be evicted. Her husband had disappeared to the pub. As they waited for the sheriff the woman asked Máirín was she married. When she was told No, the immediate response was a loud 'Ah' of disappointment. 'She felt sorry for me because I didn't have a man. Luckily, there was a positive ending, and the family was saved from eviction.'[99]

The DHAC protests continued into the 1970s and at one stage they took over the GPO, reputedly the first time it had been 'occupied' since the 1916 Easter rising. Eamonn Farrell, his wife and other protestors chained themselves to the Cú Chulainn statue before being forcibly removed by the guards. Farrell, along with some university students was charged and taken to court. The attitude of the judge to the 'College Boys' was noticeably different to how Farrell was treated. When the students were called it was a case of 'What are you studying? History, that's very interesting. Now off you go and don't do that again.' Farrell was lucky to get away with what was called 'The Standing of the Court' which meant he was ordered to

---

98   *The Irish Times*, 9th September 1971
99   The Better Side Podcast

stand until the court was adjourned. Completely unfair compared to the students but certainly better than a spell in Mountjoy prison.[100]

Shy Person

Through all these protests Máirín was a constant, determined presence. Despite her slight build and 5 ft 4 inches height, she was prepared to keep battling and never disappeared when the batons were drawn. DHAC was mainly run by men and Máirín had to stand her ground. She had no problem doing so. Eamonn Farrell now looks back on Máirín as being quite a shy person, but still she came across in a way that conveyed 'Don't cross Máirín'.

On one of their many occupations, Máirín and Farrell sat outside a house on Wellington Road, a well-off area of Dublin, keeping guard and protecting a family they had placed there. It was a known area for prostitutes to be picked up by their wealthy clients. Máirín witnessed this demeaning process for the first time and, while not shocked, she was taken aback seeing the whole sordid affair in action.[101]

Although Máirín was now in the 'pacifist wing' of Sinn Féin the DHAC were often up against private security companies who employed tough and disreputable staff to carry out evictions. In those situations it was a case

---

100 Eamonn Farrell interview
101 Ibid.

of fighting fire with fire. Máirín's joint General Secretary colleague Tony Heffernan recalls that she wasn't averse to calling on the 'military wing' of the party if she was having trouble with an eviction. That was seen to be different.[102]

Court Appearances

In the summer of 1971, there were more court appearances and a jail sentence for Máirín. This time a family had been assisted to squat in a house in Dublin's Gardiner Street and Máirín had refused to divulge the names of the family. The case ended up in the High Court and her barrister Seamus Sorohan told the court that his client "feels, as a deep matter of principle, that she cannot give the name of the squatters... She feels she must stand by them."[103]

Máirín was sent to jail for contempt of court but, crucially, there was no time limit on her term of confinement. Undeterred, Máirín and her legal team eventually ended up in the Supreme Court to challenge this decision. There one of the judges, Justice Mc Laughlin, somewhat surprisingly said that "He admired her (Máirín's) humanity and her compassionate concern for the underprivileged and her courage in sacrificing her liberty on their behalf."[104] However, he went on to make clear that he didn't approve of her occupying the premises without right.

102 Tony Heffernan interview
103 *Irish Independent*, 13th August 1971
104 *Irish Independent*, 25th July 1972

Fortunately for Máirín the three-judge court ruled 2 to 1 in her favour, with Justice Cearbhall Ó'Dálaigh and Justice Brian Walsh backing her appeal. The deciding factor appeared to be that the High Court had imposed a sentence of indefinite duration which was considered unduly harsh in the circumstances.

Máirín had won at the highest court in the land, she was out of jail but any pleasure she took from the decision lasted less than twenty-four hours. The case was referred back to the High Court the next day where Máirín was fined £200 for her contempt of court and given three weeks to pay and in default she would be sent to prison for three months.[105] Not surprisingly Máirín didn't pay the fine and in October 1972 she was arrested in her Ballsbridge flat and taken to Mountjoy jail. On this occasion Sinn Féin decided to pay the fine and she was released after two days.

The Sunday Independent reported that "Miss De Burca had indicated that she would prefer to 'do her time'. However, the feeling within the party was that she would be more useful to them if she did not serve the sentence."[106]

Endgame

The DHAC continued its protests and direct action but by the early 1970s the pressure of continuing to resist

---

105 *Irish Press,* 27th July 1972
106 *Sunday Independent,* 4th November 1972

ongoing evictions began to tell. Certainly, for the Sinn Féin activists involved, events in Northern Ireland were beginning to preoccupy them and indeed the whole country. Not surprisingly, there were some internal tensions too and accusations that the Communist Party of Ireland was trying to take over the organisation. With enthusiasm waning and the distraction of other events DHAC began to fade away and by the mid-1970s it had come to an end.

After all the protests, struggles, court cases and battles with the guards did the Dublin Housing Action Committee make a difference? The answer has to be both No and Yes. No in that DHAC wasn't able to stop the demolition of houses to make way for office blocks. Nor was it able to get local or central government to increase the supply of state housing. The Ballymun scheme had begun before the DHAC was set up and carried on regardless until it was completed by the end of the 1960s. Whether all the protests helped speed up this major project is unclear, but it seems unlikely.

During the five years of the Housing Action Committee's existence the news media were full of reports of protests, pickets and evictions. There are no reports of any meetings between the protestors and central or local government to see if they could work together and find solutions. The era of social partnership was many years away. The fault, if that's the right word, for this probably lay on both sides, but the governments of the day showed no inclination to engage in any meaningful discussions with the campaigners. It was their responsibility to take the lead.

Old comrades. DHAC members reunite in Liberty Hall C.2018.
l to r, Sean Dunne, Máirín, Eamonn Farrell. Photo: Rolling News

The answer to the question is also a Yes. DHAC certainly created huge public awareness of the capital city's housing problem. And, if only on a short-term basis, it provided families with a place to live rather than the indignity of living in a caravan or hostel. Protests such as those supporting the residents of Sara Place and Benburb Street did lead to the provision of improved housing and that was a definite plus.

The people involved in DHAC were passionate and committed and a number went on to play active roles in

Irish political life, Máirín, of course being one of them. And, almost as an add on, the changes to the Juries Act were hugely important. If there hadn't been all the housing protests, there would have been no Forcible Entry Act and no court challenge. For that alone Máirín and her colleague, Mary Anderson, should be thanked.

Fifty years on from the 1970s and the Dublin Housing Action Committee, Dublin, and indeed Ireland, is experiencing another housing crisis. In the midst of huge numbers of homeless people there are still thousands of empty houses. Máirín and her colleagues, when they reflect on all their struggles and efforts, must shake their heads in despair and wonder if some things will ever change.

6. The North Erupts

Máirín was able to take part in many of the DHAC activities as she had very tolerant employers. But housing in the 1960s wasn't the only issue to cause her to go missing from work. Protests of a different kind were bubbling up in the North and the situation there led very quickly to Máirín becoming a full-time political activist.

Civil Rights

In 1967 the Northern Ireland Civil Rights Association (NICRA) had been set up and in line with other countries across the Western world campaigns for civil rights were underway. Sinn Féin biographer Brian Feeney described the birth of NICRA in1967 as following from a seminar in Belfast which included a wide range of trade union and social interests.[107]

Máirín, however, is very clear that it was a Sinn Féin initiative. 'I remember Sinn Féin deciding to set up the civil rights movement although some people might deny it now. For the first time our party recognised that you had to deal with the majority of people who wanted to remain British, up to that we hadn't been doing this. Sinn Féin said there was a huge lack of civil rights, the level

---

107 Feeney, ch.7

of gerrymandering was appalling. The way to go was to reach out to that section of the unionist population who had concerns about human rights and civil liberties as opposed to a united Ireland. That was the birth of NICRA.'

Following on from a seminal squat in a vacant house near Dungannon, County Tyrone, a civil rights march from Coalisland to Dungannon was arranged for August 1968. Many IRA members acted as stewards on the march and 2,000 people held a largely peaceful demonstration.

A couple of months later the now famous, or infamous, civil rights march took place in Derry on October 5th 1968. Máirín travelled North with Cathal Goulding and Tomás Mac Giolla. A car breakdown delayed them and when they arrived the march was underway. Máirín went in search of the action. 'As we were late the others withdrew to a hotel. I wasn't drinking and someone said it's all kicking off in the Bogside, so I said I'm off and headed in that direction. There were barricades and I was behind the RUC and watching as the crowd tried to storm them. An RUC man called over to me, 'Ginger(my hair colour at the time) this is not a safe place for you to be'. It's funny, but any interaction I had with the RUC they always tried to protect me.'

'Later on I was watching from a doorway and another man urged me to get away. Eventually I found my way back to the hotel. They were all half cut and we drove back to Dublin in the early hours.'

A heavily policed civil rights march in Derry c.1968.
Courtesy of National Photographic Archive and Independent
Newspapers Archive.

Despite the less than active participation by Máirín's colleagues, the Derry march had a huge impact both nationally and internationally. Belfast IRA leader Billy McMillen would subsequently argue that the march had done more for the minority in the north than IRA physical violence had done in fifty years.[108]

Sinn Féin was fulsome in its enthusiastic support for the civil rights movement. In dramatic language the party described the events of 1968 as "a most stirring and exciting time in the life of the Irish people. A slumbering and despairing Irish nation has suddenly awakened and

---

108 Hanley and Millar, ch. 3

showed remarkable vigour and maturity."[109] The civil rights movement was praised to the heights and the party went on to claim, in a burst of optimism, that the "Republican Socialist ideology is the only one that can unite the mass of the Irish people both Catholic and Protestant."[110]

Burntollet Bridge

By the following year a new and more radical civil rights group, Peoples Democracy (PD), had emerged from Queens University Belfast. The Northern government had proposed some civil right reforms and some within NICRA felt they should be given an opportunity to implement them. The PD group was sceptical and organised another civil rights march for January 1969. This one was from Belfast to Derry.

The marchers were attacked by loyalists, the RUC and B Specials (an auxiliary police force) at Burntollet Bridge near to Derry city. The images of the marchers being beaten and assaulted went around the world and Burntollet became famous. That night the RUC launched an attack on Derry's Bogside smashing houses and beating civilians.

Máirín is blunt and direct in her assessment of People's Democracy. 'Burntollet was PD and I wasn't involved at

---

109 *Sinn Féin Árd Fheis Report* 1968, Tony Heffernan archive, UCD Archives
110 ibid

all. Their emergence wrecked the civil rights movement, they were putting it up to unionists. Instead of the slow steady approach we had planned they went in with all guns blazing, provoked the backlash and wrecked it. That was the end of NICRA. People's Democracy wanted to be in charge.'

Whatever about Máirín's reservations, a flame had been lit, both North and South, and it wasn't going to be extinguished. In Dublin the agitation in the North overlapped with the protests of the Housing Action Committee and other property related protests. Landlords were threatened by the IRA and in some cases had their property destroyed.

Sinn Féin continued to support civil rights protests. In contrast to the South, Cathal Goulding believed that the focus in the North had to be on winning basic civil rights before issues such as access to fisheries, land and housing could be pursued.[111] This was only partly true as discrimination in the allocation of housing in Dungannon was one of the issues that lit the civil rights fuse.

Once again Sinn Féin agonised over whether it would take part in electoral politics and end its policy of abstentionism. Seamus Costello had run as a Sinn Féin abstentionist candidate in a Wicklow by- election in 1968, getting over 2,000 votes. He was firmly on the

---

111 Tara Keenan Thomson, ch.3

electoral path and was frustrated when the party again decided against contesting the 1969 General Election.

An internal party review, led by prominent party member Sean Garland, went as far as proposing that the party should be the impetus for a 'National Liberation Front', comprising a coalition of likeminded progressive bodies. It was also suggested that the policy of not taking seats in the Dáil be dropped. The leftward trajectory seemed to be unstoppable, and then events in the North overtook Sinn Féin and everyone else.

August 1969

In the middle of August 1969 tensions between loyalist groups, nationalist communities and the RUC spilled out onto the streets of Belfast and Derry and led to some nationalist areas coming under sustained attack. It was described as a pogrom and when the nationalist people turned to the IRA for help, they encountered an organisation that was ill equipped and ill prepared. One estimate was of the IRA only having sixty men in Belfast and ten in Derry at that time.[112]

Demonstrations took place in Dublin and there were calls for the Irish Army to defend the nationalist communities. One participant at the protests recalls being told that "there would be buses at Parnell Square to bring people up to the North to fight... Hundreds

---

112 Feeney, ch 7

of people got on the buses. I realised after the buses pulled out that half of them were pissed. By the time they reached Dundalk most people had sobered up and started walking home."[113]

A perfectly sober Máirín De Burca decided she wanted to see the events first hand. 'I was at a meeting and things in the North were getting edgy. I stood up and said – On Monday I'm going to hitch to Derry does anyone want to come? This eighteen-year-old girl called Tara said she would join me. I didn't know her at all. When we arrived in Derry the army was coming in and they were being welcomed. Myself and Tara were the only ones that heckled them… We decided to spend the night in Derry but I had to get Tara to find us a place to stay, I was incapable of doing that. An elderly man took us in, gave us a big fry in the morning and we hitched to Belfast to see things there. We then hitched home. I still can't believe her parents let this happen.'

When Máirín got back to Dublin she acted immediately. 'I rang Tomás Mac Giolla straight away. I told him I was earning £13 a week in my job and if he could give me £10, I would go full time and that's how it started.' Máirín was thirty-one and Sinn Féin was to dominate her life for the next eight years.

---

113 Hanley and Millar, ch 4

General Secretary

Máirín's new job, with the impressive title of General Secretary, came at a time of national turmoil. Some politicians in the South were calling for weapons for northern nationalists and people were flooding back into the IRA. At one point Seamus Costello and Cathal Goulding approached Michael O Riordan from the Communist Party of Ireland asking if the Russians could supply weapons.[114]

Although working full time for the party, Máirín wasn't directly involved in any of the attempts to get guns and arm republicans. Somewhat surprisingly, despite the trip North which prompted her to work full time for the party, it wasn't to be her priority. 'I wasn't that exercised about the North. It wasn't my major preoccupation. There were enough people focusing on that and it was never held against me.' Máirín had moved toward pacifism and as she explained it to herself 'If you go into politics and you support physical violence and you are wrong then people die. If you don't support physical violence and you're wrong at least people don't lose their lives and you're not hurting anybody.'

While not fully active on the Northern issue, Máirín took whatever opportunity she had to fearlessly condemn the use of physical force, particularly by the IRA. At a public meeting outside the GPO in Dublin in 1970 she

---

114 ibid

deplored the fact that "six Irishmen had been shot in Belfast, possibly by Irishmen who considered themselves Republicans. She emphasised that Republicanism was neither Catholicism nor Protestantism and never had been."[115] Although clearly controversial, Máirín was not stopped by Sinn Féin from making such statements.

Máirín continued to support the civil rights movement and went North every weekend for a year to join its different protests. Once again she was brought into contact with helpful RUC men. 'I used go with my friend Hughie from Lurgan ... once we were coming into this town and we didn't know where our march was. We approached a barricade and asked an RUC man. He lowered his voice and said 'I'll lift this barricade and you two get across the square as soon as possible', obviously we were at the wrong march.'

The pair set off across the square and then Máirín lost the run of herself. 'I said to Hughie, I'm going to Paisley's march, I want to hear what he has to say. I was up at the front and then realised I was being isolated. I heard someone say 'Fenian bitch'. Hughie said to take one step back at a time and they let us out. When we got back to the car, which was untouched, I asked him 'Can they really tell the difference between Catholics and Protestants?' He just looked at me and said, 'Next time take off your James Connolly badge.'

115 *The Irish Press*, 1st Jul 1970

Throughout the second half of 1969, tensions were simmering in Sinn Féin between hard core, physical force republicans and those members who wanted to continue the party's more left-wing approach. It was all to come to a head at the party's 1969 Árd Fheis, which took place in January 1970. Máirín, however, was also preoccupied with other matters.

The South African Springbok rugby team was to play against Ireland on the same day as the Árd Fheis. As the full-time secretary Máirín had made all the arrangements for the event and had decided to go first to the protest against the Springboks in Lansdowne Road and then back to the nearby Intercontinental Hotel for what was due to be a crucial Sinn Féin gathering. In terms of her standing in the party it wasn't the most astute move for Máirín to miss part of their annual Árd Fheis, but as her colleague Tony Heffernan reckoned, "That would be her. I think this is more important and damn the consequences."[116]

Home Visits

In this busy world of politics and activism Máirín had little time for visiting her family in Newbridge. She would go home the odd weekend and for two weeks in the summer, mainly because she couldn't afford anything else. But home was not a happy place and the death of her parent's first son Patrick continued to be a dark

---

116 Tony Heffernan interview

shadow that never went away. 'It took so much out of them. Their first child and a boy at that. Daddy was a very affectionate man but that knocked any affection out of him. My instinct is that Daddy worshipped his little boy.' And as for her mother. 'She was an unhappy woman at that stage. Life didn't turn out well, losing the child was the start and it went downhill after that.'

Sinn Féin Split

Máirín missed the first half of the Árd Fheis, where momentous events were taking place within the party. A long debate concerning the idea of a 'National Liberation Front' ended with that concept being supported. However, the proposal to end abstentionism didn't get the necessary two thirds majority. It was a close-run thing and 'the abstentionists', having seen the way the wind was blowing, had already decided to act.

In a pre-arranged move, hard core republicans, led by Ruairí Ó Brádaigh and Seán Mac Stíofáin, left the Árd Fheis and declared they were setting up a new organisation. It was to lead to the birth of Provisional Sinn Féin. (The IRA had split the previous month and the Provisional IRA emerged as a result).

While many were very upset at the 'split', Máirín had few reservations. 'I remember sitting there watching them walk out and I wasn't sorry to see most of them going... The split was about the armed struggle and about the left-wing shift in the party. They didn't like the way the party was moving. I wanted them gone. We all wanted them gone.' *The Irish Times* described it as a "division on right and left-wing ideologies." One delegate told the paper that those who walked out were 'Fascist sectarians.'"[117] The new Provisional Sinn Féin in a statement said that, in addition to their views on abstentionism, they were unhappy with "the extreme form of socialism being pushed on the Movement."[118]

Máirín was less than happy to learn that, in her absence, she hadn't been re-elected as general secretary (a separate position to her full time job). It was a petty decision in response to her prioritising the Springbok protest. 'They knew where I was and at the end of the Árd Fheis there was a meeting of the new Árd Comhairle and after twenty minutes they came out and said they were going to co-opt me; they had made their point.'

By the time the following year's Árd Fheis came around Máirín's party, now known as Official Sinn Féin, had moved on and was by then committed to contesting local government elections in the South and to formally registering as a political party. Máirín told the party delegates "that it was essential that local elections were contested before a general election or a by election." Seamus Costello went much further declaring that the

---

117 *The Irish Times* 12th January 1970
118 Feeney, ch.8

party's job "as a revolutionary movement was to organise mass agitation.[119]

The move to embrace democratic politics was a big step for the party. Alongside that, Seamus Costello's radical views were undoubtedly sincerely held by him and his many other left leaning colleagues. The problem was that events in the North during those difficult years often pushed politics and radical ideas in the South far into the background.

Most Terrible Decade

Sinn Féin historian Brian Feeney has described the 1970s as "the most terrible decade in Ireland in the twentieth century ... over 2,000 people died as a result of the Troubles."[120] There were now two parties, Official and Provisional Sinn Féin and two military wings- Official IRA ('The Officials') and Provisional IRA ('The Provos'). Cathal Goulding was Chief of Staff of the Officials with Seamus Costello Director of Operations.

Máirín's reaction to the split was to intensify her political and anti-sectarian activities in Dublin. 'I decided to saturate Dublin with posters from us. We had a very good artist, Rory Corrigan, and a trio of us went out night after night, I was carrying a bucket of paste on my scooter. The posters were anti sectarian and pro working class. One

---

119 *The Irish Times*, January 18th 1971
120 Feeney, ch 8

of them simply read 'Guns Kill Workers'. People used ask us for them as souvenirs. We needed to highlight Official Sinn Fein as an anti-sectarian party.' Máirín's contact with the North in the early 1970s continued to be minimal, confined primarily to her attendance at the weekend civil right marches.

The Provos with their simple message began to take the lead position in working class nationalist areas in the North. The Official IRA, which had been run down during Cathal Goulding's time in charge, were becoming less relevant. They did mount their own operations and often disputed with the Provos over who was responsible for which attack. And sometimes they fought with each other. Just like the Civil War fifty years earlier, republican fighting republican became common.

A press release from Official Sinn Féin in March 1971 condemned the situation where "Irishmen attacked other Irishmen with guns and other weapons while their main enemy the forces of British Imperialism looked on with satisfaction." The statement went on to highlight the number of incidents where their members had been assaulted while selling the party paper *The United Irishman* and other literature.[121]

Under the calm leadership of Tomás MacGiolla, Official Sinn Féin tried to move beyond all the republican

---

121 Irish Republican Publicity Bureau, Press Release, 13th March 1971, Tony Heffernan archive, UCD Archive

infighting. In his address to the 1970 Árd Fheis MacGiolla said that the party "refused to be distracted into futile arguments and controversies with former comrades" and endeavoured to concentrate its "most bitter attacks on British imperial interests and their supporters in this country." However, MacGiolla also felt the need to state that "There is … clearly one legitimate Sinn Féin organisation and this is it."[122]

The growth in support for both the Provos and Officials was unwittingly aided by the British government when they introduced internment in August 1971. There was huge public condemnation and both the Officials and the Provos saw a large increase in membership. The Officials justified robberies by claiming that the money was being used to advance the cause of socialism.[123]

Bloody Sunday

Anti British sentiment was further enhanced when fourteen people were killed by the British Army in Derry during 'Bloody Sunday' at the end of January 1972. Bloody Sunday led to a huge backlash, North and South, and became an issue which infected Irish-UK relations for the next forty years. The British Embassy in Dublin was burned down a few days later, with Seamus Costello a central figure. It seemed that large scale civil unrest in the South was on its way.

---

122 President Address, Sinn Féin Árd Fheis 1970, Tony Heffernan archive, UCD Archives
123 Hanley and Miller, ch.5

Where was Máirín De Burca during these momentous events? In Dublin, dealing with immediate housing problems. 'By the time of internment and when the North blew up I had lost interest. It wasn't a priority as I would have been too involved in social issues in the South... I was terrified of another large-scale military campaign and I didn't want hand act or part in it.'

The burning of the British Embassy in Dublin after Bloody Sunday. 1972.

While the political situation in the North was often on the brink of major conflict, Máirín remained determined to keep her focus on social issues and the party's left-wing ideals. In a somewhat dramatic interview she gave to the *New York Times* in 1970 she was described as a "smallish, determined woman of 32, dressed in dark jeans and a white Aran-knit sweater." She described Official Sinn

Féin as a "revolutionary threat to the state… I'm not interested in blowing up customs posts on the border, if the only objective is to enlarge the republic, I don't have an hour's time for that."[124]

It was stirring stuff, but it reflected a deep rooted opposition on Máirín's part to political violence and a consistent desire to promote social change. Small in stature she might have been, but this was a woman unafraid to put her head over the parapet.

On the day of Bloody Sunday Máirín was on a picket in Drumcondra in Dublin supporting a woman who was about to lose her home. "There was a woman with a small child being evicted. There was snow on the ground, and it put things in perspective for me."[125]

'My priority was that woman. I would have cared about the North but I made a choice to get involved in social issues and I would have no argument with those who did get involved in the North. It didn't cause conflict in the party. I did make anti- military speeches and no one in Sinn Féin stopped me saying anything I wanted to say.'

Máirín continued to be resolute and unafraid in her condemnation of the Provos or any suggestion that Unionists would be forced into a united Ireland. Speaking in Derry in 1971 she said that the republican movement "has never and will never ask or coerce any

---

124 *The New York Times*, 12th December 1970
125 *The Better Side* Podcast

Irishman, Protestant or Catholic, into an enlarged Free State."[126] The following year she called for bombing attacks to stop, insisting that "This will do nothing but polarise our community further and lead to a sectarian civil war. In the name of humanity this bombing must stop immediately."[127]

After one of her speeches condemning violence in the North, one letter writer to the *Evening Herald* said that Máirín had shown "a rare kind of courage by speaking out as she did. We can applaud that courage by letting it be seen that there are many who hold the same views but lack the opportunity- and possibly courage - to voice them."[128] It was genuine praise from just one person but there is no doubt that many others supported those sentiments. Máirín's approach was echoed by her party which continued to call on the Provos not to engage in a campaign of violent revenge.

Aldershot Bombing

Unfortunately, this appeal fell on deaf ears, both within the Provos and the Officials. In February 1972, in response to the Bloody Sunday killings, the Official IRA bombed the headquarters of the British Army Parachute regiment in Aldershot, killing five women cleaners, a chaplain and a gardener. "When the news came through about the

---

126 *Irish Independent*, 12th April 1971
127 *Strabane Chronicle*, 8th April 1972
128 *Evening Herald*, 1st November 1974

bombing Máirín was in a pub where everyone around her cheered."[129] She didn't and instead was very upset. 'That was a dark time. I didn't have anyone to go to about it. It's hard to understand when you're not part of it… we kind of tolerated each other and left each other alone.'

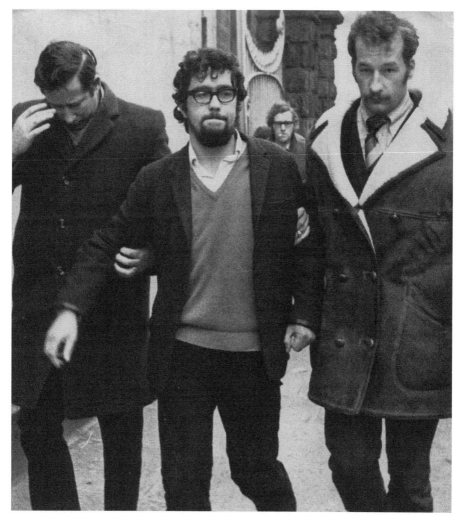

Márín's colleague, Tony Heffernan, being arrested after the Aldershot bombing. 1972

129 *The Irish Times* Podcast

After Aldershot Máirín's former colleague in the DHAC, Hilary Boyle, challenged her pacifism in an open letter in *The Irish Press*. Boyle noted that Máirín had "very often announced that you are a pacifist (but wondered if Máirín) knew what real pacifism involved." She went on to suggest that after Aldershot Máirín "became an accessory after the fact and as guilty as those who actually placed the bomb."[130] Boyle concluded by challenging Máirín to a public debate. It was strong stuff but no more trenchant than criticism Máirín herself meted out to many individuals and organisations.

Could or should Máirín De Burca have walked away from Sinn Féin at this stage? A debatable question but she didn't resign and continued to promote her pacifist views inside the party. Reflecting on these events Máirín's rationale was, 'I would have thought you don't change anything by flouncing out... I could have flounced out but why would I? I respected the people in it too much to do that...I stayed in and contributed to getting them away from the gun.'

Three months later, at the end of May 1972, the Official IRA announced an indefinite ceasefire stating that they were doing this to avoid a descent into full scale sectarian civil war. Many years later, reflecting on the thirty years of conflict, Máirín is clear in her belief that "anything that was achieved- and what was achieved? - could have been achieved without one death."[131]

---

130 *Irish Press*, 3rd March 1972
131 *The Irish Times* Podcast

Official Sinn Féin continued its leftward trajectory in the midst of violence, ceasefires and more violence. The policy of abstentionism was ended in 1971 and the party backed the legalisation of contraception and the introduction of divorce. Common place policies now, but quite radical in the 1970s. At an international level, Máirín attended conferences in Jordan and Kuwait to discuss the issue of Palestine.

American Visa

In 1972 Máirín had hoped also to conduct a speaking tour to the USA but her visa application was rejected. In their letter of refusal the State Department wrote that Miss De Burca had been convicted of crimes of moral turpitude (a dictionary definition cites 'depraved or wicked behaviour') and claimed her activities endangered the safety of the United States.[132]

Many years later Máirín accessed her FBI file, albeit heavily redacted, and the attitude towards her in the US security system was laid bare. The file, of over 150 pages, is an extraordinarily forensic record of Máirín's activities in Ireland, and in America when she was allowed in a few years later. It was evident that Máirín was being closely watched by the US Embassy in Dublin.

In cables from Dublin back to the State Department, Máirín was variously described as a "Well known Militant

---

132 *Irish Independent*, 6th October 1972

Irish Extremist Left Winger", a "well known communist figure" and the "Republic's leading woman political agitator." Rather dramatically she was described as a "romantic nationalist at 16 (who) is now a well-known fanatic."[133] In a way Máirín must have been pleased but surely questioned how they ever knew what she believed as a sixteen year old teenager?

```
 IRELAND                                              '
                                          UNCLASSIFIED
 Mairin (Maureen) DE BURCA               RPT. May 13, 1971

     Joint Secretary of the "Official" wing of Sinn Fein
 and Republic's leading woman political agitator. One of
 small group of communists who have sought to infiltrate
 and gain control of the Irish Republican Movement. Born
 about 35 years ago in Newbridge, Co. Kildare, where she
 attended convent school.  Later lived in Bray, Co. Wicklow
 and now in Dublin.  A "romantic nationalist" at 16, now a
 well-known fanatical agitator once described in a press
 interview as "sarcastic, sharp-tongued, stubborn, gritty
 and sometimes severe." Contemptuous of organized religion
 and believes "all property is theft."  Prominent in a wide
 variety of communist-inspired nationalist protests, demon-
 strations and agitation.  Violently anti-U.S.; threw egg at
 President Nixon in Dublin in Oct.1970 and burned flag at
 U.S. Embassy Dublin in April 1971.  Has several times
 visited Arab guerrillas in Middle East, presumably for
 training in revolutionary techniques.  Unmarried.
                                                  Dublin.
```

Extract from Máirín's FBI file, where she is described as the Republic's leading female political agitator. De Burca papers.

The fact that Sinn Féin also held an 'Anti Imperialist Festival' in Ireland in 1974 further upset the US Embassy in Dublin. Máirín's file claimed that she had "several times visited Arab guerrillas in the Middle East, presumably for training in revolutionary tactics."[134]

---

133 FBI File, De Burca archive
134 Ibid.

It noted also that in her visa application Máirín wrote that the purpose of her visit was to see a friend. But the Embassy was able to point out that Máirín's speaking engagements had already been advertised in America. The Irish guards helpfully provided the Embassy with information on nine separate instances where Máirín was up in court on various charges.

After all that it was no surprise that the Embassy recommended the visa application be rejected which it duly was. After this refusal Máirín called to the Embassy to retrieve some documents and, while she was there, tore down a poster and then ran out of the building. This behaviour was also dutifully reported to 'Head Office' in Washington. It was 'payback time' for the American security system who had watched carefully Máirín's political activity and in particular her active involvement in anti-Vietnam war protests in Dublin.

The early 1970s was a hectic period for Máirín. There was her new job, with a national political party to manage; there was the housing crisis and there was the North. Describing her as being busy and committed at this time is an understatement. But, on top of all that, she somehow found time to help start a vibrant women's liberation movement.

7. Liberating Women

Máirín's range of causes was wide and impressive. Often they overlapped and the same people wore a number of different campaigning hats. There was Housing and Vietnam, Apartheid and Prisoners' Rights. It is probably fair to say that at, or near the top of the list, was the liberation of women. As a woman and a social activist, it was inevitable that Máirín would get involved in challenging the many inequalities women endured in 1970s Ireland.

When people look back on the setting up of organisations, it is often hard to identify what was the 'First' – the first gathering, the first event, the first public statement. However, there is a general consensus that Máirín De Burca was a key figure in the establishment of the Irish Women's Liberation Movement (IWLM).

Mary Maher

In the late 1960s the ground had begun to be prepared. In 1967 Mary Maher, a radical and feminist journalist from Chicago, introduced a 'Women First' page to *The Irish Times* and started to write about contraception, unmarried mothers and deserted wives among many other topics. This was something completely new and within a few months the other national dailies, *The Irish Press* and *Irish Independent*, had followed suit.

All of a sudden there was a national platform for women's issues. In 1968 Pope Paul VI unwittingly lent a hand. His Papal Encyclical *Humanae Vitae* was resolutely opposed to contraception and provoked protests across the world, including in Ireland; the times were indeed changing. The Fianna Fail Government, with Jack Lynch as Taoiseach, appointed a Commission on the Status of Women in March 1970. Its brief was to examine and report on the status of women in Ireland and to make recommendations on how women's participation in society could be enhanced.

In the summer of 1970 some American feminists visited Máirín in the Sinn Féin offices and spoke about contraception and other women's issues. They spoke of the civil rights movement in America and its radicalising effect. However, they also pointed out that it was the women in these movements who were still left to 'make the tea and lick the stamps.' That had started them on the road to creating a movement specifically for women.

Bewleys Meeting

Máirín had already been reading about the movement in America and was primed for action. After a short stay in prison for a minor offence, 'I had decided I was going to pursue equal rights for women. You do have plenty of time to think in there and I had time to solidify my thinking. Mick O'Riordan from the Communist Party said to me when I came out – 'You're not into that nonsense are you?'. But she certainly was.

Her first move was to ring her friend Mary Maher who was clearly on the same wavelength. Apart from her feminist views and her groundbreaking journalism, Maher was left wing in her politics and an active trade unionist. Following their phone conversation, they arranged to meet with three other women - Margaret Gaj, Máirín Johnston and Dr. Moira Woods in Bewley's Café in Dublin. It was the summer of 1970 when this formidable group of active and committed women got together.

Restaurant owner Margaret Gaj, more commonly known as 'Mrs Gaj', was known to Máirín via the DHAC and other campaigns. Máirín was also a regular customer in her café as were many others on 'the left' in Dublin. Máirín often recalled that she could always rely on Mrs. Gaj to bail her out of jail, no matter what the hour.[135] Future IWLM activist Rosita Sweetman reckoned that "There's always somebody and some place in every city who looks after the poets and artists and maybe the druggies and the politicos, and Mrs. Gaj was that person."[136] Máirín Johnston, from Dublin's Liberties, was a long standing left wing activist and member of the

135 Anne Stopper, *Monday's At Gaj's: The Story of the Irish Women's Liberation Movement* ch.1 (The Liffey Press, 2006)
136 ibid

Communist Party and brought a wealth of campaigning experience to the group.

The final member of that 'Group of Five' was Dr. Moira Woods who stood out from the others. Married to another doctor and living on Dublin's exclusive Ailesbury Road, Máirín regarded her as "having an aura of respectability that… (I) lacked but that proved useful in many situations."[137] Despite her place of residence, or maybe because of it, Moira Woods had a strong commitment to equality and civil rights issues. She was also an active member of the anti-Vietnam War campaign.

After their initial meeting in Bewley's things moved quickly. On October 13th 1970, 'We then had a meeting in Mary Maher's little house, we were feeling our way. We were very hesitant, and it was ages before we had a public meeting.' The meeting had to be held in Maher's house as she had no childcare to call on, which was indicative of the issues Irish women had to deal with.

Mondays at Gaj's

With an increasing level of interest, meetings were transferred to a weekly gathering at Mrs. Gaj's restaurant and 'Mondays at Gajs' became the place to be for progressive women in Dublin. Many of the original founders were regular customers already. Máirín, with her political and campaigning experience, knew how

---

137 Stopper, ch.5

to organise and others involved saw her "as a pillar of logic and common sense." Mrs. Gaj believed that Máirín was "one of the cleverest and most committed of all the women in the IWLM."[138]

Other journalists and activists such as Nell McCafferty, Mary Anderson, Rosita Sweetman, Mary Kenny, Marie McMahon, Mary Sheerin and Eimear Philbin Bowman quickly got involved. One of the rules at the meetings in Gaj's was that no one was to bring any food. That was a stereotype that had to be broken.

For hard working Máirín it was another of a series of meetings in a busy day. There was a regular meeting in the Sinn Féin offices every Monday evening and then she would dash over to Gaj's to catch the latter half of the women's gathering. Máirín arrived too late for what was called the 'consciousness raising' part of the meeting where participants would talk about more personal aspects of their experiences of being a woman in Ireland. Consciousness raising was seen to create a "bond of sympathy between these women with different educational backgrounds and political affiliations."[139]

Topics such as domestic violence, masturbation and contraception were discussed and often written about by the journalists involved. Rosita Sweetman found these sessions one of the most important things that the women's movement brought to Irish politics.[140] However,

---

138 Stopper, ch.2
139 Stopper, ch.4
140 Rosita Sweetman interview

Máirín wasn't so sure that she needed to engage in discussions about how she felt when she first saw a penis.

'When the meeting was over, they would tell me what happened and then they would go off for a drink. I was often tired after a very long day and just wanted to go home. I missed some of the debates but Sinn Féin was my prime interest, and this was secondary.' Indeed, her colleague Tony Heffernan recalls some people in Sinn Féin complaining "that if she devoted as much time to organising the party as she did to that bloody women's thing we would be a lot better off."[141]

Naming Feelings

The discussions in Gaj's were lively, rowdy and sometimes chaotic. However, as the Movement's biographer notes, the women there were "naming the things that, although they may have been invisible to most of society, were preventing them from being free, equal citizens – their own feelings, the country's deeply ingrained patriarchal attitudes, the oppressive laws. It was in this way that the IWLM began its real work towards women's liberation."[142]

For many of the women involved it was a time of hope. For Rosita Sweetman, who worked on *The Irish Press* women's page with Mary Kenny, it was a joyful time. "I was twenty-one and everything was fun… we went out and made the news and then wrote it up… we were the

141 Tony Heffernan interview
142 Stopper, ch.5

first people to challenge the power of the Catholic church head on."[143]

This formidable group adopted the name of the Irish Women's Liberation Movement (IWLM). The new organisation had the distinct advantage of having the three editors of the national Dáily newspapers' Women's Pages as leading members. The three editors - Mary Maher in *The Irish Times*, Mary Kenny in *The Irish Press* and Mary Anderson in the *Irish Independent* - were determined their pages weren't going to be filled with cookery recipes. Issues of concern to the IWLM featured regularly.

Key Demands

Side by side with the emergence of the IWLM the Irish government, as an aspiring member of the European Economic Commission (EEC), was under pressure from Brussels to deal with the issue of equal pay. The Commission on the Status of Women recommended in 1971 that equal pay for like work be phased in over a five-year period. The government now had to deliver.

In the summer and autumn of 1970 each of the national newspapers carried articles on the women's liberation movement, with *The Irish Times* giving a whole week to the subject. Rosita Sweetman recalls that the women's editors "were intent on not just upsetting the old apple

---

143 Rosita Sweetman interview.

cart, but also dumping the apples and the cart in the ditch and creating something new."[144]

By the end of 1970 the IWLM had crystallised their thinking into six key demands. These were:
- Equal pay
- Equality before the law
- Equal education
- Contraception
- Justice for deserted wives, unmarried mothers and widows
- One family, one home.[145]

The last of these was always going to be controversial with some women regarding it as 'socialist' and not strictly a 'women's issue'. For Máirín it was a key concern. 'We tried to keep politics out of it and some people didn't like the 'One Family, One Home' demand but we got it through. That was seen as political.' Máirín argued bluntly that you can't talk about freeing women from the kitchen sink if they haven't got a sink in the first place. 'I said the people who suffer from homelessness are women. I had been to several evictions where men took off to the pub before the Sheriff arrived.' Máirín was not a woman to be messed with and she made sure the housing issue remained centre stage. The issue of equal pay was also a crucial demand for Máirín. Given her trade union

144 Rosita Sweetman, *Feminism Backwards*, p.111/112 (Mercier Press, 2020)
145 Pat Brennan, *Women in Revolt* in *Magill*, April 1979

background and the unequal pay she experienced as a female worker, it had to be near the top of her list of demands.

Chains or Change

By the beginning of March 1971 the IWLM had clarified its position on a number of issues crucial to women and produced its detailed policy document *'Irishwomen: Chains or Change'*. While the one family - one home issue didn't appear in *'Chains or Change'* it remained one of the Movement's key demands. Then twenty-one-year-old Sweetman recalls, "there were the older sisters and the younger sisters. They seemed to know everything, and we seemed to know nothing." She regarded Máirín as "very serious and very determined. A really unusual person, quite scary as well."[146] With the help of Marie McMahon's typesetting business 7,000 copies of *Chains or Change* were printed and distributed.

June Levine, one of the prominent IWLM activists, recalls in her memoir the concerns of some in the Movement that Máirín was getting them involved in politics. Máirín responded bluntly, "They'd be right, we are involved in politics. We're trying to change the things that affect people's lives, that's as political and revolutionary as you can get."[147] However, one political

---

146 Rosita Sweetman interview

147 June Levine – *Sisters: The Personal Story of an Irish Feminist*, ch 6 (Ward River Press, 1982)

issue the IWLM successfully steered clear of was the North. It just wasn't discussed and didn't form any part of their public statements. It was seen by those involved as a wise decision.

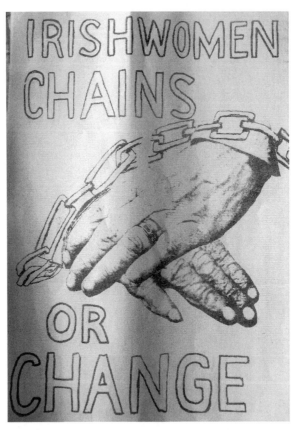

Front cover of Chains or Change. 1971. Courtesy Rosita Sweetman.

The thirty-one page *Chains or Change* document was a mine of information although it was presented in a dense and difficult to read format. It was subtitled 'The Civil Wrongs of Irishwomen' and outlined in forensic detail the discrimination experienced by Irishwomen. However, some issues, such as rape, abortion and lesbianism were seen as a bridge too far at this time and weren't referred to in the document.

Chains or Change outlined that under the law women couldn't serve on juries; in employment they were paid less than men; in education girls couldn't study the same subjects as boys; in the family there was no divorce and no contraception; and in taxation a woman was treated as an appendage to her husband.

The IWLM finished its document with the heading *'Five Reasons To Live In Sin'*, where they highlighted the fact that if you weren't married you could keep your civil service job, you would be better off tax wise, you could manage your own bank affairs and you could remain an independent woman rather than the 'property' of the husband.

The Late Late Show

It was a comprehensive analysis and the IWLM were now ready to take their case to the public. Máirín and Mary Maher, two of the most prominent members, wanted to proceed slowly and not frighten other women away with an aggressive public campaign. However, events overtook them when Ireland's premier TV programme *The Late Late Show* came calling.

The flamboyant and well-connected Mary Kenny casually announced to a Monday night meeting in Gaj's that they had an opportunity to appear on *The Late Late*.

She got a mixed reaction ranging from 'Who does she think she is' to excitement at the opportunity. Sweetman, who describes the hot pants wearing Kenny as a woman "with a cigarette holder out to here and a feather in her hat out to there", thought it was a brilliant idea despite a number of the women being very cross.[148]

Mary Kenny had the advantage of being well known and was always ready to make an eye-catching comment. She was also something of a liability. Máirín's concerns were expressed in a later interview when she said that "If you want to denigrate an organisation you go after its wackiest member, don't you?"[149]

Apart from Mary Kenny, Máirín was also concerned about how women in rural Ireland might react. "We were a rural society to a great degree at the time, but a lot of very conservative rural women still felt hard done by… there was no point in racing ahead because we were half a dozen young progressive women in Dublin. You had to try and bring them along with you, or what was the point." She urged caution regarding *The Late Late* and didn't want to be overtaken by the 'mad phase' of Mary Kenny.[150]

Despite this hesitancy most members of the IWLM regarded an appearance on Ireland's premier TV programme as a great opportunity to highlight their cause. The show took place on March 6th 1971 and was completely devoted to the women's issue. Máirín

148 Rosita Sweetman interview
149 Stopper, ch. 8
150 Stopper, ch. 6

Johnston and Nell McCafferty represented the IWLM on the panel and they also got the more 'respectable' faces of Irish feminism to appear- then barrister Mary Robinson, RTE producer Lelia Doolan and historian Mary Cullen, the latter being introduced as the 'wife of a psychiatrist'.

Máirín didn't fit into the 'respectable' category and sat in the audience along with others such as Rosita Sweetman and Mary Kenny. The women on the panel got an opportunity to set out their stall, highlighting the various ways in which women were treated as second class citizens. And then the fireworks began. Mary Kenny from the audience challenged the failure of politicians to end this wholesale discrimination against women. June Levine shouted that 'You don't have to be black in Ireland, you only have to be a woman'. Máirín complained about the soon to be introduced Forcible Entry Bill. The show took off and host Gay Byrne struggled to keep control.[151]

Prominent Fine Gael TD and future Taoiseach Garret Fitzgerald had been watching the programme at home and rushed out to RTE to defend himself and other politicians. As Máirín recalls, 'He was agitated and felt they hadn't been given credit for the things they had done... Nobody minded him doing that; it gave us publicity you couldn't buy.' Looking back on the show Máirín was able to see its benefits. "I suppose in the long run it didn't do us any harm. Once it was out, it was out and you couldn't haul it back in again."[152]

---

151 Pat Brennan, op cit, Magill
152 Stopper, ch. 9

Other protests followed, with a series of demonstrations in a number of Catholic churches at the end of March gaining more publicity. The occasion this time was a letter from Archbishop McQuaid, condemning contraception, being read at Sunday masses. McQuaid's missive stated that "Any contraceptive Act was always wrong in itself." When this was read out during mass at the Pro-Cathedral in Dublin eight women and one man walked out, with one saying "This is absolute rubbish."[153]

Across the city on Dublin's southside Mary Kenny wasn't to be outdone. At mass in Haddington Road church, she stood up and declared, "This is a wicked pastoral. It is disgraceful and contrary to *Humanae Vitae*. This is church dictatorship." Alongside her, Máirín Johnson also stood up and said, "This is a matter that should be decided by women alone. Why should men dictate to us how many children we should have?"[154] Kenny and Johnson then walked out of the church. Women standing up at mass and speaking out about contraception? This was something really different.

Mansion House

With the massive publicity arising from *The Late Late Show*, the IWLM was ready to hold its first public gathering. With some nervousness they hired the Mansion House in Dublin for a meeting to take place

---

153 *The Irish Times*, 29th March 1971
154 Ibid.

on April 14th 1971. The journalists involved with IWLM used their papers to advertise the event.

Cautious Máirín was unsure. 'We had no idea how popular it would be. We said let's take the Mansion House and if six or six hundred come that's ok. It was jammers, people were upstairs on the balcony, standing everywhere and we knew we were on the right track. I spoke briefly but there were far more interesting contributions from women who weren't active.' Rosita Sweetman stood with her eyes on stalks as she watched women queueing around the corner to get in.[155]

IWLM members Moira Woods, Máirín Johnson and Mary Maher, spoke from the platform, with Nell McCafferty chairing proceedings. There were many more speakers from the audience and in the end over sixty women, and some men, addressed the large gathering. Many of those queuing to speak missed out when the three-hour meeting ended at 11pm.

One of the unknown speakers, a woman called Helen Heaphy, captivated the meeting. She stood at the microphone and asked the audience how many of them were unmarried mothers. After a pause she said- 'I am one myself and I am very proud of my little daughter.'

Heaphy's contribution was regarded as a seminal moment with Nell Mc Cafferty writing later, "That

---

155 Rosita Sweetman interview

single sentence was our epiphany. You could see, feel and hear the dam break. It could not but help that she was relatively mature (all of about thirty years old), lovely looking with it, dressed in gypsy style, and had an authentic Dublin accent. Helen never spoke publicly again."[156] Máirín recalls 'She brought the house down as no one had said that publicly before.'

Ironically, the success of the Mansion House meeting also led to difficulties within the Movement. How was such a large grouping to be managed? Who were the leaders and who was in charge? Nearly one thousand women had attended the Mansion House meeting but the IWLM was not fully prepared to channel all this energy in a coordinated manner.

Local Groups

Those who attended the Mansion House were invited to join local groups based on their postal district and these groups then set out to respond to the issues that concerned them. It sounded sensible in theory but difficult to coordinate in practice. Twenty-eight local groups were set up and the founders of the Movement then proceeded to try and get these groups to accept the 'key demands' as presented in *Chains or Change*. However, not everyone was on the same page The group in Donnybrook, in Dublin 4, for example, had a

---

156 Nell Mc Cafferty – *Nell*, ch 15 Penguin Ireland, 2004)

particular difficulty in accepting the 'one family, one home' demand.[157]

It took just two weeks from the Mansion House event for another issue to emerge. There was discontent about the suggestion that a women's liberation contingent be organised to attend the traditional May Day march. Those concerned argued again that such a march wasn't strictly a 'women's issue', whereas those on 'the left' saw protesting against the treatment of women in the workplace as an essential concern. These debates were to surface constantly during the IWLM's brief existence.

Magazine published by the Fownes St. local IWLM group.1971.
De Burca archive.

157 Tara Keenan Johnson, ch. 5

In the end about 300 women joined the May Day parade "many pushing prams or carrying children in arms… the women carried placards with slogans demanding equal pay, equal opportunities, day nurseries for children and increased social benefits."[158] After the march Máirín was one of the speakers. She challenged the trade union movement to organise its members against the Forcible Entry Bill and wanted to see mass organisation of workers. If trade unions didn't do this Máirín claimed "they will be betraying the working class as they have so often done in the past."[159]

The IWLM did not have any kind of committee structure, nor a chairwoman, as they didn't want any hierarchy. Sweetman reflects that "We weren't a political group, we were a think tank group. We didn't have the wherewithal to keep it going as a political movement."[160] A lot of new women started to attend the Monday night meetings and there were some suggestions that the founders were controlling and arrogant.

Contraceptive Train

Notwithstanding these tensions the Movement decided their next challenge was the high profile and vitally important issue of contraception. On May 16th 1971 a meeting was held in Dublin's North Star Hotel and the leadership group, drawing on their media and public

158 *The Irish Times,* 3rd May 1971
159 ibid
160 Rosita Sweetman interview

relations savvy, decided to organise a 'contraceptive train' to go to Belfast and return to Dublin with a variety of contraceptives, all of which were banned in the South.[161]

Forty-seven women set off for Belfast along with TV cameras from Britain, Japan and America. There were only a few Irish journalists on the train. It was May 22nd 1971, World Communications Day, and the IWLM were intent on delivering a strong message. However, despite their bravado many of the women had the same thought– 'What will our mothers think.'[162]

Máirín decided not to travel. 'I said I wouldn't travel. I explained that if we want to attract women from rural Ireland then a single woman buying condoms is not the way to go. I said I would organise the reception when they came back.' Before the train headed for Belfast Máirín had argued that only married women should go. In the end it was left up to each woman to decide and a number of single women, such as Mary Kenny and Marie McMahon, got on board.[163]

Perhaps more surprisingly, Máirín also had mixed views on the issue. "Personally, I believed that sex was to be shared exclusively between married adults. I know it dates me for saying it and nowadays it sounds silly but at the time it was a real issue."[164]

---

161 Tara Keenan Johnson,, ch.5
162 Stopper, ch 14.
163 ibid
164 Ibid

For her part Rosita Sweetman missed the morning train which left from Dublin's Connolly station at 8 am. "Bad me, I wasn't one of them. It was my twenty third birthday and I stayed in bed with my man... Ironically, since he was English, he had plenty of contraceptives .... Nell (McCafferty) still says ' You stepped out of history, Rosita.'"[165] Sweetman, however, was there when the train returned.

Rosita Sweetman, who missed the contraceptive train,
as she was 'otherwise occupied' that morning.
She was there to welcome the train on its return.

The forty-seven women piled off the train in Belfast and Nell Mc Cafferty described in hilarious detail their visit to a chemist in Belfast. First, she asked for 'The Pill' and was told she needed a prescription. Undaunted, she ploughed ahead requesting coils, loops, diaphragms and anything

165 Sweetman, op cit p.149

else that came to mind. Mc Cafferty was determined to return with 'The Pill' and resorted to buying packets of aspirin guessing that the customs officials in Dublin weren't going to scrutinise them too carefully.[166]

For her part Marie McMahon was embarrassed to be told by the chemist she was too young to buy contraceptives. She was twenty three at the time.[167] The older June Levine was appointed as the expert in such matters and was plied with questions such as, 'What does gossamer mean?', and 'What do you do with this jelly stuff?'[168] On the way back to Dublin some of the women became anxious, but Mary Kenny both entertained and annoyed passengers by blowing up condoms and letting them off in the carriages.

Welcome Home

Back in Connolly station in Dublin Máirín had done a good job in organising a lively welcome and a few hundred women comprised a large 'reception committee'. Máirín had been anxious to make sure there was a good turnout. 'I said I would organise the reception coming back. I told them you'll have a very good welcome home. The biggest anti-climax would be having risked arrest to find there was no one to welcome you back. That would have been awful. I got hundreds and it was very effective.'

166 Nell Mc Cafferty, ch. 15
167 Ibid.
168 June Levine, *Sisters*, quoted in Nell McCafferty, ch 15

Máirín also made sure there was a large media presence and there was huge publicity as a result.

When the women marched down the platform they challenged the customs men, popped aspirins into their mouths and threw condoms over the railings. Máirín Johnston went up to the customs officials told them she had spermicidal jelly, but they weren't getting it. The unfortunate customs officials didn't know what had hit them – literally.

Nineteen-year-old John O'Connor was all of two weeks in his job as a customs officer when he was sent to Connolly station that day. "There was a big crowd I remember… I was told to stand at a table and I asked, 'What are we looking for?' I was told we were seizing condoms and I said, 'What are they?' O'Connor was told to "stand there and look intelligent. I was also told to smile because there were cameras on us, so I just smiled like a Cheshire cat."[169]

It was a party atmosphere and Máirín and the welcoming crowd chanted 'Let them through, let them through.' Rosita Sweetman recalled watching the woman getting off the train. "Standing at the station and seeing them come down the platform towards the gates… my heart was pounding, and I was thinking, the revolution is coming and there is absolutely no doubt about it."[170]

169 *Journal.ie*, 10th April 2017
170 Stopper, ch 13. s

Defiant IWLM members returning to Connolly station in Dublin after their 'shopping trip' to Belfast.1971. Courtesy National Photographic Archive and Independent Newspapers Archive

Nell McCafferty remembers, "We waved our contraband and challenged the guards to come out and arrest us - with Máirín De Burca there, I, for one, was willing to face tanks. However, the police would not come out to play."[171] After they left the train station some of the more confident women headed for nearby Store St. Garda station 'to make a formal complaint about Fionnuala O'Connor being thumped by a guard.'

---

171 ibid

Real Concerns

Despite the carnival atmosphere some of the women had real personal concerns. Marie Mc Mahon was so worried about her mother's reaction that she arranged for her sister to visit home that evening to distract Mrs. McMahon from watching the news. Máirín Johnson, who confronted the customs officers, was very worried as she was pregnant, that she could end up in jail. Nell Mc Cafferty put it in this way, "we considered the three most important facts of life, all of them above and beyond contraception - What would our mothers say? What would our editors say? Would we still have our jobs?"[172] No one was reported to be sacked or thrown out by their mothers, but real bravery and determination were shown by the women that day.

There was widespread national and international coverage of the event. The IWLM issued a statement where they challenged the hypocrisy of a government which allowed so many thousands of women to use 'the pill', ostensibly as a cycle regulator. That night Mary Kenny and another member, Colette O'Neill, appeared on *The Late Late Show* to highlight the issue. Once again, the IWLM had brought a crucial issue for women to national attention.

The whole carnival atmosphere of the day wasn't universally applauded. Some members thought the behaviour and antics (take a bow Mary Kenny) on

---

172 MC Cafferty, ch 15

and off the train were undignified and diminished the seriousness of the issue. However, that one day is seen as making a significant impact on creating awareness of the need for the whole issue of contraception to be addressed.

The Contraceptive Train was a huge 'political' and public relations success. Ironically, it was also the IWLM's last public event.

Dáil Protests

The availability of contraception continued to be a key demand for the IWLM and there were regular protests outside the Dáil demanding government action. On one such protest, Rosita Sweetman recalls "a red-faced bully emerged from inside the Senate chamber shouting, 'Ye should all be fucked on your hands and knees like animals because that's all ye are."[173]

At about the same time as the women received that foul abuse, Mary Robinson, now a Senator, had been attempting to get a Contraceptive Bill debated. Máirín and her colleagues, Fionnuala O'Connor, Marie McMahon and Hilary Orpen, were picketing the Dáil to lend support. Frustrated with the lack of response the women got into the Dáil grounds, saw an open window and climbed inside. It turned out to be the men's toilet. 'The guards raced down the stairs and started thumping

---

173 Sweetman, op. cit, p.121/122

people around. One of the TDs, it was either Niall or David Andrews, appeared and said he would bring us to the visitors' room. In a very civilised fashion, he sat us down and we discussed the whole pros and cons of contraception.'

In a press interview after this protest Máirín gave a sanitised version of events. "We had gone in to see three senators to ask them to explain why the contraceptive Bill did not get a reading in the Seanad." She didn't mention that 'going in' consisted of climbing through a toilet window. In the same press interview Máirín made clear that "We intend to continue with our protests until contraceptives are legalised."[174]

After leaving, or being ejected from, the Dáil, to the chants of 'We shall not conceive', the next stop was Pearse St. Garda station. Máirín wanted to make a complaint about one of her colleagues being assaulted by a guard during the arrest. 'There were two guards, one of them taking my statement and the other being awkward and interfering. One of them told me - 'You don't need contraceptives, you can use the rhythm method.' 'I explained that's fine for women who have a regular menstrual cycle, but most women don't. Whereupon the awkward one piped up - 'She's dead right you know.' When we came outside, we laughed and I thought, there's a guy who has had a failed rhythm method experience.'

---

174 *Irish Independent*, 1st April 1971

While there was the occasional smart comment in Sinn Féin about burning bras, Máirín got support from the Party President Tomás Mac Giolla. There was a 'cabal' in the party who opposed resolutions to party conferences on the subject just because Máirín was involved. However, Mac Giolla was different. 'Tomás would have read the literature, knew what you were talking about and was there at your back. There was one women's resolution at an Árd Fheis and as I supported it 'they' were all against it. Tomás took them by surprise when he stood up and supported it and it was passed. That's why I had such great respect for him.'

Fennell Resigns

Despite the huge publicity generated by the Mansion House meeting and the contraceptive train there was trouble ahead. In June 1971 Nuala Fennell resigned from the Movement. Fennell was a high-profile member who later went on to become a Fine Gael TD and Minister of State. She had always been wary of some of the more radical members of the IWLM, the hot pants wearing, pipe smoking Mary Kenny being a notable example. As a mother with three young children, Fennell felt removed from the lives of some of the single IWLM activists. Nor was she impressed by the contraceptive train and felt that some women were being alienated by the 'antics' on that day and at other events.

In her letter of resignation she wrote, "I can no longer work for these changes with an elitist and intolerant group who are using Women's Liberation as a pseudo-respectable front for their own various political ends, ranging from opposition to the Forcible Entry Bill to free sedatives for neurotic elephants." She concluded by stating that "if you are not anti- American, anti-clergy, anti-government, anti-ICA, anti-police, anti-men, then sisters, there is no place for you either."[175] Fennell claimed also that the IWLM was essentially a middle-class organisation, with its leading members trying hard not to show it. That claim particularly annoyed Máirín and colleagues such as Máirín Johnson and Marie McMahon.[176]

Nuala Fennell's broadside was a scathing condemnation of her colleagues and of a movement that had achieved a lot in less than a year. Some IWLM members hit back with letters to the national newspapers. Máirín Johnston noted that Fennell had been present at the meeting which supported the one family - one home policy and she couldn't see therefore how Fennell could then complain about the IWLM's opposition to the Forcible Entry and Occupation Bill.[177]

Forcible Entry

The issue of the Forcible Entry Bill was a live one in the summer of 1971 and its passage in the Dáil was the issue which led to Máirín being arrested and her subsequent successful challenge to the constitutionality of the

---

175 Stopper, ch 12.
176 ibid
177 ibid

Juries Act. A large number of IWLM women joined in the protests against the Bill outside Leinster House. However, participation in this type of protest continued to be a divisive issue with some of the 'feminists' in the Movement again suggesting that housing and 'Forcible Entry' weren't strictly their concerns.

Once more concern was voiced over what was seen as the undue influence of left wing and republican groups. This continued dispute was an important factor in the Movement's eventual demise. To copper fasten its position the IWLM in February 1972 approved a resolution supporting only non-violent means in support of its aims.[178]

The local groups set up around Dublin had varying levels of success. The Baggot Street group allowed for male members and that was another source of friction. There were continued accusations that the IWLM was made up of 'dissatisfied middle class hussies' and to counteract these suggestions Nell McCafferty went to meet a group of women in Ballymun every week. She described it as a chastening experience. "They were broke, some had marriage problems and none of them had the fare into town, never mind a train fare to Belfast. We were spending more time trying to help the women get welfare benefits and money for bills than we were spending just meeting them on Monday nights. It was hard and sad going and I fell by the wayside."[179]

---

178 Ibid
179 McCafferty, ch 15

Moving On

In an effort to create some form of coherence Máirín and the other founding members decided that their meetings in Gaj's would just be for them so that they could act as the movement's executive. Inevitably, there were charges of elitism and exclusion.[180] By the autumn of 1971, just a year after IWLM was set up, many of the local branches were struggling and a lot of women had dropped out. By the end of the year only one of the local groups continued to operate.[181]

Alongside these difficulties, a number of the key founders were moving on, some quite literally. Mary Kenny went to London to work for the *Evening Standard* which led Rosita Sweetman to describe her as a traitor and a turncoat.[182] Máirín was a lot more forgiving when Kenny also became more conservative in her outlook. "She changed her mind, big deal"[183] was her simple summary.

Mary Anderson went to live in America and Nell McCafferty headed to France. Mary Maher had two small children and her job in *The Irish Times* to occupy her. Sweetman herself later moved to live in Africa, not wishing to stay with *The Irish Press*, which was changing the Women's Page, after Kenny's departure. Both Mrs Gaj and Moira Woods had husbands who were unwell to

180 Pat Brennan, op. cit. Magill
181 Stopper, ch.15
182 Sweetman,, p.155
183 *The Irish Times* Podcast

care for. And Máirín had plenty to be doing in her 'day job' with Sinn Féin.

Success Story

The IWLM lasted for just over a year, but in its brief lifespan it did make a real difference. Issues affecting women were brought on to the public and political agenda and they never went away, even if it took many more decades for all of them to be properly progressed. Many, many women experienced change in their own lives. When the publicity and debate generated in the Mansion House, by *The Late Late Show* and by the Contraceptive Train is considered, there must have been many thousands of women whose eyes and minds were opened by these never seen before events. It was all truly groundbreaking.

Máirín is clear in her opinion about the Movement's impact. "The women's liberation movement was a success story. I don't care what anyone says, it was a success story. I have been in a lot of organisations that have split from time to time, but this was a nice split. The women's movement didn't stop… It went on. They (the founders) saw where they wanted to go and they went off and did it. All the things they founded are still there."[184]

---

184 Stopper, ch. 16

IWLM members at the launch in 2006 of 'Monday's at Gajs' by Anne Stopper which describes the work of the Movement. L to R. Eimer Philbin Bowman, Rosita Sweetman, Máirín, Rosheen Callender(sitting),Mrs. Gaj, Mary Sheerin, Marie McMahon (sitting), Máirín Johnston. Photo: Derek Speirs.

Many years later Mary Maher recalled that when the IWLM ended she was outraged and upset... (but then she) gradually realised that this is history and this is the way things happen. It (IWLM) served its historical purpose."[185] The ever-pragmatic Máirín De Burca is sanguine about the demise of the IWLM. 'Various women went off to do different things. Nuala Fennell set up AIM (an advocacy and advice group for women), Maura Richards set up Cherish (a support organisation

---

185 Tara Keenan Johnson, ch 5

for single parents), Nell set up the Irish Women United (a radical feminist organisation). Various women's organisations came out of it and I thought that was good. Nuala, Gemma Hussey and Monica Barnes all got elected, all for some reason known only to God stood for Fine Gael. Weird wasn't it?'

Trade Union Women

After the demise of the IWLM, Máirín and Mary Maher, the two 'politicos' in the Movement, continued their interest in the role of women in the workplace. A trade union women's forum had been formed with Rosheen Callender, the first non-secretarial female employee in the Irish trade union movement, as one of its founders. Callender was employed by the ITGWU and had a keen interest in equality issues. She found Máirín to be "dynamic and a wonderful activist."[186].

Although Michael O' Leary from the Labour Party was the Minister for Labour there was concern he would 'have his ear bent' by employer groups on the equal pay issue. The trade union forum lobbied and held protests to make sure that the 1973-77 Coalition government of Fine Gael and Labour didn't seek a derogation from the EEC rules.

A trade union colleague of Callender's from America, Debbie King, was visiting Ireland and showed the Irish women a direct approach to getting the Minister's

---

186 Rosheen Callender interview

attention. King had met Michael O'Leary at a party and the next day she attended a meeting of the women's forum. "She couldn't understand why we were being so low profile. So, she rang the Department of Labour, insisted on speaking to the Minister, claiming she was a personal friend and that she needed to speak to him immediately. Eventually she got through to O'Leary and proceeded to berate him for his lack of action on equality issues for women and efforts to seek a derogation from the equal pay directive. We sat there with our mouths open. She was a dynamo, another Máirín De Burca."[187] What influence Debbie King and the Trade Union Women's Forum had is unclear, but Ireland did proceed to implement the equal pay directive via various pieces of legislation introduced in the mid-1970s.

Make Up Dilemma

While the women's issue was a deadly serious one for Máirín and her colleagues, there was also time for the occasional piece of frivolity. In 1975 *The Irish Times* asked Máirín and a number of other women what type of make-up they used. With her usual honesty Máirín said "I don't approve of make-up. I think what a woman looks like should be irrelevant."[188] She went on to admit that she sometimes used mascara and used face cream, "the cheapest there is, because I ride a motorbike and

---

187 ibid
188 *The Irish Times,* 22nd October 1975

the cream keeps the wind from tearing my skin off."[189] In further 'dramatic revelations' she disclosed that she also used lipstick but would never dye her hair. Máirín finished the interview in a typical self-deprecating manner when she said, "I don't think there is a make-up invented that would improve the face God gave me."[190]

It was a light hearted exercise and Máirín entered into it in that spirit while also making some serious observations. However, the issue of women's equality was a very serious one which Máirín prioritised both inside and outside of Sinn Féin for the rest of her career. She campaigned and wrote about it whenever she could. It was and is an essential part of her true 'make up'.

The first few of years of the 1970s saw Máirín in her 'protesting prime'. Between the housing action committee and the women's movement she was constantly on the streets and regularly in trouble. In a five-month period, between May and September 1971, she variously appeared in court over the Gardiner Street squat, took part in *The Late Late Show* on the women's issue, protested outside the Dáil about the Forcible Entry Bill, helped organise the seminal Mansion House women's meeting, climbed into the Dáil over the contraceptive issue, arranged the reception for the contraceptive train and took on the state over the Juries Act.

---

189 ibid
190 ibi

149

And if that wasn't enough, she also found time to engage in important international issues.

8. International Struggles

Both Máirín and Official Sinn Féin saw it as important to have a focus on international issues. Máirín had a particular interest in Palestine and she had travelled abroad to discuss the issue and met with Yasser Arafat, the Palestine Liberation Organisation (PLO) leader. The party had also been represented at international events where the struggles of other nations were discussed. Back home both Máirín and the party were particularly active on two key international issues - apartheid in South Africa and the war in Vietnam.

Máirín meets with PLO leader Yasser Arafat in Lebanon.
c.1973. De Burca archive.

Apartheid

Challenging the Apartheid regime was a key concern of left wing and progressive movements in Ireland from at least 1960. That year African and Irish students set up the 'Anti-Apartheid Committee' and picketed the Shelbourne Hotel in Dublin where the Springboks rugby team was staying before its match against Ireland.[191]

It was the beginning of decades of protests against the apartheid regime. The Irish Anti-Apartheid Movement (IAAM) was founded by Kader Asmal, a South African lecturer in Trinity College Dublin (TCD). It was to become one of the most vocal protest movements in the Western world and it faced an uphill struggle. Soon after it was set up, the IAAM in November 1964 had to call on the Irish government to support a United Nations (UN) motion calling for economic sanctions against South Africa. Two years earlier, Ireland along with Britain, was one of 16 nations who voted against a UN motion on the issue, with 51 countries voting in favour.

Máirín and Kader

Máirín was the Sinn Féin nominee to the IAAM and, as ever, she threw herself into the Movement. Asmal was a charismatic figure and saw himself as the undoubted leader of IAAM. However, Máirín did not always see

---

191 *Evening Herald*, 16th December 1960

eye to eye with him. Máirín felt that Asmal dominated their meetings and there was little interaction with the members. On one occasion she brought her knitting to a meeting to make the point.

Asmal, while wanting to see protests taking place, was also keen to distance himself from direct action. 'He maintained deniability. If we wanted to paint slogans, he would give us money for the paint but he wouldn't do the painting. If anyone got annoyed with a slogan, as they did, he could say 'that was the youngsters.' Máirín was in her 30s at this time.

She also had concerns about Asmal's overall political views. 'Kadar was a closet communist and a supporter of the Provos. Conor Cruise O Brien (a human rights activist and Labour Party politician) was one of our sponsors and his name was on our headed notepaper, along with others such as Lord Killanin (head of the Irish Olympic Committee). Kader came to one meeting to say he wanted to remove Conor's name as he didn't support the armed struggle. Myself and Joan Burton (future leader of the Labour Party) challenged him. I said if that's the case we should write to all our sponsors and see if they also support the armed struggle. Kader didn't want that and eventually backed down. He targeted Conor because he was anti – Provo.'

Despite these differences the IAAM was successful in consistently highlighting the apartheid issue whenever they could. They opposed any sporting contact with South Africa and in 1965 when the Springboks were back again to play rugby, the IAAM led the protests. The President, Eamon De Valera, and a number of government ministers did not attend the match.

The following year the IAAM objected to another sporting competition between Ireland and South Africa. This time it was boxing, and the thrust of the approach was to condemn South Africa to sporting isolation. In 1968 the Movement broadened its horizons and protested against the British and Irish Lions rugby tour of South Africa that summer. Their protests fell on deaf ears as seven Irish players joined the tour, with Irish full back Tom Kiernan selected as captain.

Rugby Tour

Rugby was South Africa's main sport, and its government was anxious to maintain competitive links with other countries. The planned Springboks visit to Ireland in late 1969/early1970 became a major source of conflict and protest. The IAAM had called for the tour to be cancelled but the government was not inclined to block the invitation extended by the IRFU.

The rugby fraternity rallied round their decision. The President of the Irish Rugby Football Union (IRFU), JWS Irwin, said "people are perfectly entitled in making protests if they have to, but I don't think they represent the majority of people in the country... For these South African people to see how black and white people can live here peacefully can do nothing but good."[192]

Greystones and Palmerston rugby clubs said they wouldn't make their pitches available to the South Africans for training, not for ideological reasons, but because they were afraid of damage by protestors. Most of the other clubs seemed happy to follow whatever the IRFU decided, and Lions captain Tom Kiernan said, "I will go to the match. I don't think anyone will agree with apartheid – but there are different opinions as to what we can do about it. Should one not play with them and trade with them?"[193]

With the government and the IRFU supporting the tour, the IAAM mounted a formidable campaign of opposition and Máirín, of course, was right in the thick of it. She and her IAAM colleagues went to the airport on January 7th 1970 to 'welcome' the Springboks and got hauled away from blocking their bus. Máirín was hurt and ended up 'bleeding for South Africa.'

The next challenge was to find out where the team was staying. Máirín and a young colleague (a judge later accused her of leading him astray) went on Máirín's trusty Vespa scooter to Wicklow and eventually tracked the team down to the Royal Starlight hotel in Bray.

192 *The Irish Times,* 7th November 1969
193 *Ibid*

'We put on an all-night show, blowing whistles so they wouldn't get any sleep.'

The Post Office Officials Association said "when we find out the hotel, we will give the telephone number to all exchanges and see that it is not serviced. Similarly, no mail will be delivered."[194] *The Irish Press* reported meeting a burly Springbok forward who said that "this is the worst they've ever been. Even in Swansea they never stayed outside all night."[195] The hotel was under siege, with a huge Garda presence and barbed wire added to fences.

However, Máirín and her colleagues didn't have it all their own way. An opposing group outside the hotel chanted 'Sinn Féin out' and 'Springboks welcome.'[196] Even the local clergy weighed in to support the visiting team. 'One of our mass-going colleagues told us that a local priest denounced us, saying that we should be supporting our kith and kin.' The protests turned nasty and there were a number of bomb hoaxes. In the course of the all-night vigil a member of Sinn Féin, Eamonn Cahill, was arrested and charged with possessing a petrol bomb.[197]

Fine Gael TD, Dr Hugh Byrne, had welcomed the South Africans and offered to show members of the team

---

194 *The Irish Times,* 5th January 1970
195 *Irish Press* 8th January 1970
196 ibid
197 ibid

around Leinster House. As a result his house was picketed by members of the Labour Party and the IAAM. One of the banners read 'Fine Gael's Enoch Powell'. In response Dr Byrne said that if the match was cancelled it would be "a blow against the freedom of individual organisations and the individual in society."[198] The picket only lasted a couple of hours as the protestors had to get ready for the match.

Anti-Apartheid protestors outside Lansdowne Road before the Ireland v South Africa match. 1970.

On the day of the game Máirín and her colleagues splattered the Springboks coach with paint as it drove to Lansdowne Road. A large protest march led by the IAAM left Parnell Square in the city centre and made its way to the venue. The protestors, who numbered about 6,000, had decided not to try and enter the ground and

198 *The Irish Times*, 9th January 1970

all they could do, amidst a large Garda presence, was whistle and throw pennies over the wall. Then Máirín had to rush off, back to Sinn Féin and that momentous Árd Fheis where Provisional Sinn Féin came into being.

After the match the protests continued, outside the Shelbourne Hotel where the team was staying and the Royal Hibernian Hotel where the IRFU was hosting the after-match dinner. It is unlikely Máirín was able to get away from the Árd Fheis but if she did she would have been in the middle of a nasty battle, with the protestors throwing stones, bottles and eggs and the guards responding with a baton charge.

Inside the hotel it was quite different. *The Irish Times* reported that "the Springboks and the Irish team moved around freely and over drinks they joked and laughed about the demonstrators outside… at the IRFU dinner there were speeches complimenting the South Africans on their sportsmanship, claiming the protests outside were not really representative of Irish society."[199]

When the meal was over the players got ready to leave. One of the Springboks players, after looking at the protestors, said, "they should be drafted into the army so they could get a haircut." To which one of the Irish team responded by saying, "If this crowd of weird bastards touch us I will tear them to pieces."[200]

---

199 *The Irish Times*, 12th January 1970
200 ibid

Máirín's colleague, Des Geraghty, was active in the IAAM, and with difficulty marshalled one of the protests. Kader Asmal, who Geraghty describes as a 'bit of dictator', came along and started telling people where to picket. One protestor took offence at this and asked 'who's that black bastard telling us what to do.'[201] Luckily, this comment didn't become public at the time.

The Springboks played their final match in Limerick where they were met at the train station by a much smaller protest, led by future TD Jim Kemmy. The 'Boks' won their match against Munster and finally headed home. The level of protest against the South Africans over their short visit was huge and it certainly raised the awareness of many Irish people about the evils of apartheid. In contrast, the attitude of the Irish rugby establishment, even by the standards of the 1970s, was simply appalling. They really did show their true colours.

The work of the IAAM continued through the 1970s and they kept the pressure on regarding any sporting contacts with South Africa. In 1973 the Movement protested about an Irish hockey team playing in the South African games and even complained about two farmers from Rhodesia (now Zimbabwe) taking part in the world ploughing championships in Wexford.

Rugby continued to be a contentious issue and there was widespread opposition to any Irish player joining the

201 Des Geraghty Interview

1974 Lions rugby tour to South Africa. Not surprisingly, the objections were rebuffed by the IRFU who said, "that many of those who attack us have wider political motives." In response the IAAM described the IRFU's position as "self-righteous, defensive and pathetic."[202] It didn't make any difference as eight Irish players went on the tour, with Irishman Willie John McBride appointed as captain.

In 1976 Steve Biko, one of South Africa's most inspirational activists, was brutally assaulted and killed in custody. Máirín wanted to know what the IAAM planned to do about it. Apart from the outrage of his death it was an opportunity to highlight the brutality of the South African regime. However, there were no protests from the IAAM. 'We did nothing, and do you know why? Biko wasn't a member of the Communist Party, he was aligned with some other group that Kader didn't approve of... so we did nothing.'

Apartheid Ends

Máirín continued her involvement in the IAAM after she left Sinn Féin in 1977 and took part in their many protests and campaigns. After many years of struggle Nelson Mandela was released from jail in 1990. That year he came to Ireland to receive the Freedom of Dublin city and to thank the Irish people for their support.

---

202 *The Irish Times,* 27th March 1974

Given these changed circumstances, Máirín raised the issue at an IAAM meeting and said she thought it was time for the African National Congress (the main anti-apartheid movement in South Africa) to end its armed struggle. 'Kader turned on me and said – 'You don't know what you're talking about.' Two weeks later the ANC announced it was ending its armed struggle.

Despite these differences, Máirín regarded her involvement with the anti-apartheid struggle as positive and on this occasion she was eventually on the winning side. In 1994 Nelson Mandela became the first black South African president and Kader Asmal was appointed a Minister in his new government. Whatever about any disagreements they had, Máirín was pleased for Asmal. 'I thought it was fantastic. When you think of him not being able to go home because he was married to a white woman… He was dying to go home. I was so chuffed for him.'

Vietnam

The war the United States waged in Vietnam during the 1960s and 1970s provoked condemnation from people around the western world. The 'Irish Voice on Vietnam' group had been started by veteran republican and socialist Peadar O' Donnell and Máirín became an active member. She was the Sinn Féin delegate and didn't always get full party support with one member asking, in true Monty Python style, - 'What has Vietnam ever done for us?' Despite this, Máirín was passionate in her opposition to the war. Vietnam, she felt, defined her generation. "I remember being so, so passionate about it. I would have done anything to try to stop it. I would have done anything."[203]

While Official Sinn Fein in Ireland was very much against the war, there was opposition to this stance from their supporters in America. They questioned whether Sinn Féin was now becoming 'Communist'. Members of Cumann na mBan were hostile to this new direction for the party and made their objections public.[204] After 'the split' Máirín and Official Sinn Féin's involvement gave an opportunity for Provisional Sinn Féin to highlight the radical policies of their counterparts, often shouting at them to 'Fuck Off back to Vietnam.'

Street Marches

There was, however, considerable public concern about the war with regular street marches, protests and public meetings in Dublin from the mid-1960s onwards. It was an issue on which various left-wing groups - republicans, communists and socialists - could work together. In 1967 Tomás Mac Giolla spoke at a public meeting in Dublin's Abbey Street (Ireland's 'Speakers Corner') and complained that Ireland "had made no effort to organise opinion of other small nations in a move to end the

---

203 Stopper, ch.2
204 Des Geraghty interview.

Vietnam war. All Irish political parties must take the blame as none had taken a definite stand."[205]

The following year the Irish Voice on Vietnam handed a letter in to the US embassy in which it likened the war to what had happened to the Irish people, with the US playing the role of imperial Britain.[206] Máirín's friend Dr Moira Woods made a point of contacting every bishop in the country asking them to denounce the war. On one occasion Wynns Hotel in the centre of Dublin claimed they were duped into allowing a pro- Vietcong meeting in their hotel. The meeting was reserved in the name of a 'Dr Woods.'[207]

Irish Voice on Vietnam on one of its many protest marches in Dublin. C.1970

205 *The Irish Times*, 5th July 1967
206 *Sunday Independent*, 24th March 1968
207 *Sunday Independent*, 22nd March 1970

One of Máirín's many protests was to disrupt a concert in Dublin's Jurys Hotel hosted by the Irish American Society. Guests arriving to the hotel in evening dress were handed leaflets by the anti-war demonstrators. Somehow Máirín got into the concert room and as the music played Máirín, the 'uninvited guest', started to read from the leaflet detailing the horrors of the war. She was quickly removed but told a reporter afterwards, with her tongue firmly in her cheek, that "It was beautiful."[208]

Máirín didn't always see eye to eye with Peadar O'Donnell, the Irish Voice on Vietnam's leading figure. She was inclined to do 'solo runs', sometimes bringing her pot of paint with her. In May 1970 she was up in court for daubing an American bank in Dublin's Grafton Street with the slogan 'Murderers - USA'. Helpfully, when put into the police car, Máirín told the guards they should also go to the American Express office where they could see another example of her 'artwork'.

When the case came to court Justice O'Huadaigh said that "Miss De Burca was clearly the ringleader in this matter" and sentenced her to two months in jail.[209] The only surprise was that the judge wasn't on first name terms with Máirín given she was such a regular visitor to his court. Over the course of the next year Máirín fought this sentence all the way to the High Court and then to the Supreme Court. Indeed, on June 17th 1971 Máirín

---

208 *The Irish Times,* no date
209 *Irish Press,* 23rd June 1970

had the distinction of having her case mentioned in the District, High and Supreme Courts on the same day.[210] Her grounds were primarily technical as the Judge had made the mistake of recording a three month sentence in his records rather than the two month one he actually gave. Eventually, Máirín lost in the Supreme Court but managed to avoid the jail sentence.

Peadar and Máirín

In Peadar O'Donnell Máirín again came up against a man who wanted to dominate the organisation. And Máirín wasn't good at taking direction from anybody, especially when she disagreed with them. 'Peadar was somewhat dictatorial. The guards would say – don't block the main road and he wouldn't let us.' However, Máirín's colleague Des Geraghty saw O'Donnell as someone with "a good theoretical view…he had a picture of what the way forward was."[211]

O' Donnell was a good organiser and in October 1968, as part of world-wide demonstrations, a protest march was held in Dublin from Parnell Square to the American Embassy in Ballsbridge. O'Donnell involved republican folk hero Dan Breen in an effort to attract support, especially from Fianna Fail members. About 1,000 people took part, carrying a coffin labelled 'child killers', which they dramatically threw into the river Liffey at

---

210 *Irish Independent,* 18th June 1971
211 Des Geraghty interview

O'Connell Street bridge.[212] Máirín, of course, was an active participant. Protestors in Dublin did everything they could to highlight their opposition to the war. On another occasion demonstrators stopped the showing of an American film called 'The Green Berets,' which depicted the war in Vietnam, and had to be removed by the Gardai.[213]

After the shooting dead of four anti-war students in Kent State University, Ohio, in May 1970 there were further international protests. 'We decided to have a public meeting and the guards said – don't block the main road. We said – sorry the whole point is to block the road. No way were we going to be pushed around. Peadar resigned when we decided to continue. I spoke at the meeting and the guards told me that as a result of my speech they thought the crowd was going to storm the US embassy.' The protests expanded to include opposition to America's invasion of Cambodia. Once again Sinn Féin spoke out and claimed that "The expansionist policy of American imperialism is now completely revealed by their blatant invasion of Cambodia."[214]

Nixon Visit

President Richard Nixon came to Ireland in October 1970 and his visit entailed large scale security, which involved restricting air traffic, closing some roads and

212 *Irish Times* 14th and 15th May 1968
213 *Irish Independent,* 24th June 1970
214 *The Irish Times,* 2nd May 1970

a travelling party which included up to 100 American secret service men.[215] Despite this, it was a golden opportunity for Máirín and her colleagues to again highlight their opposition to what was happening in Vietnam. A mock 'trial' of the President took place (he was found 'guilty') and an effigy of Nixon was burned outside the US embassy in Dublin, with 250 guards in attendance.[216] One newspaper headline suggested Nixon was impressed by his 'warm welcome'.[217]

Máirín was determined to make an impression and on this occasion her weapon of protest was – eggs. Along with her colleague Martin O'Hagan (later killed by a Loyalist group in 2001) she headed into Dublin city, bought six eggs and they took three each. Máirín was well known to the guards at this stage and disguised herself with a scarf and sunglasses. They knew the route the President's cavalcade was to take; she headed for the Quays and O'Hagan went to Dublin Castle. Máirín didn't regard herself as a marksman (woman?) and was very pleased when her eggs splattered directly on the Presidential windscreen. Security officers were heard to shout 'It's all right, it's only an egg'.[218]

A guard on duty told *The Irish Press* that he had to pull Máirín away to safety as the crowd were so angry, with someone shouting, 'throw her in the river'. Another

---

215 *The Irish Times*, 3rd October 1970
216 *The Irish Times*, 5th October 1970
217 *Irish Press*, 5th October 1970
218 The Better Side Podcast

woman ran across the road and tried to hit Máirín.[219] For her 'bullseye' Máirín was fined £2. Other charges such as using threatening words and resisting arrest were dismissed.[220] Martin O'Hagan was also convicted for his egg throwing but only received a £1 fine. It was surprising that Máirín didn't appeal the injustice of her excessive punishment.

One year later, a further demonstration outside the US Embassy in Dublin resulted in Máirín serving six weeks in jail. Another day of international protest had been arranged for April 24th 1971 and the Irish group decided on something dramatic. 'I got animal blood from a friendly abattoir, and we spilt it outside the Embassy. It looked very effective although the smell was terrible. One of the lads took down the American flag and burnt it. There were no guards there and we could have got away but I said No, we need to picket.'

Eventually the guards arrived and Máirín and ten of her colleagues were arrested and then charged with defacing the property. However, a US marine had to identify the people actually involved in the flag burning and he could only point the finger at Marie McMahon, Máirín, Martin Gaffney and his American wife Gorenka.

Máirín's charge sheet read that she "did wilfully prevent the exercise of the right conferred by the Diplomatic

219 Stopper, op cit, ch.2
220 *Evening Herald*, 17th November 1970

Relations Act 1967 to use the flag of the United State of America on the said premises."[221] The case came before the District Court in October 1971 and the end result was a three-month jail sentence for all four accused. Half the sentence was actually served.

```
(                    -------------------       122182
O 241700Z APR 71
FM AMEMBASSY DUBLIN
TO SECSTATE WASHDC IMMEDIATE 2601
INFO AMEMBASSY LONDON IMMEDIATE

UNCLAS DUBLIN 408

S E C O N D  C O R R E C T E D  C O P Y  (MRN 408 VICE 0114)

LONDON FOR RSO

1. AT 3:50PM LOCAL TIME GROUP OF SEVEN MALES, THREE FEMALES
LED BY MAIRIN DE BURCA WELL-KNOW PRO-COMMUNIST FIGURE WALKED
UP STEPS TO CHANCERY MAIN DOOR WHICH LOCKED VIEW OFFICE CLOSED.
THEY WERE CARRYING "GET OUT OF INDO-CHINA" PLACARDS AND HURLED
BLOOD ON DOORWAY AND STEPS AND LANDINGS BETWEEN STEPS.
ALSO CUT HALYARD OF FLAG POLE HAULED DOWN AMERICAN FLAG SOAKED
IT IN KEROSENE AND SET FIRE TO IT. MARINE GUARD ON DUTY TELE-
PHONED ADMINISTRATIVE OFFICER WHO ARRIVED AT 4 PM WHILE GROUP
WERE PICKETING. HE RECOVERED FLAG WHICH CHARRED BUT NOT
TOTALLY BURNED. THREE POLICE SQUAD CARS ARRIVED AT SAME TIME
RESPONDING TO TELEPHONE CALL FROM MARINE GUARD. POLICE CON-
SISTED OF ONE SUPERINTENDENT, TWO SERGEANTS, SIX PATROLMEN.
POLICE SENT FOR POLICE VAN AND TOOK ENTIRE GROUP INTO CUSTODY.
WE RECOGNIZED SOME OF THEM AS HARD-CORE ANTI-AMERICAN AGITATORS.
DE BURCA WAS THE PERSON WHO ASSAULTED PRESIDENT'S CAR WITH
EGGS.

CHIEF SUPERINTENDENT WHO ALSO VISITED CHANCERY ADVISES
AMBASSADOR THAT GROUPS WILL BE HELD IN CUSTODY FOR WEEKEND
AND CHARGES WILL BE PREFERRED PROBABLY MONDAY DEPARTMENT OF STATE A/CDC/M
MOORE
              UNCLASSIFIED        REVIEWED BY _____ DATE 3
                                  RDS ☐ or XDS ☐ EXT. DATE_____
                                                    REASON(S)
```

An extract from Máirín's FBI file describing her involvement in the burning of the American flag. De Burca archive.

For her protest outside the Embassy Máirín received support from the American National Peace Action

---

221 District Court Papers, 13th October 1971, De Burca archive.

Coalition. They sent a message to say they stood "in solidarity with Máirín De Burca, joint general secretary of Sinn Féin, political arm of the IRA."[222] It might have been gratifying for Máirín to receive this backing, but it certainly wouldn't have helped her application for a visa to go to America in subsequent years.

Jail Time

Jail was extremely difficult for Máirín. "Prison was one of the worst experiences of my life. I had never, ever been unfree. I was single and always wanted to be single and live alone. I have loner's inclinations. Suddenly you weren't alone, and you weren't free."[223]

However, even in jail Máirín was in fighting form. 'The second in command in the jail was a bit of a pain. Every morning we were expected to stand at our door and queue to empty our chamber pots. I decided to wait in my cell until the queue was over and I heard a voice roaring at me to stand in the doorway. We had got a copy of the prison rules and knew there was nothing about standing in the doorway. The whole place was silent and in a very quiet voice I said to her 'If you wish to speak to me, you may do so in a normal voice. I am not deaf.' There was more silence, she struggled to respond and then walked away.' It was a small but important victory.

---

222 *Irish Press*, no date
223 ibid

The next morning Máirín and her colleagues wanted to go out for exercise and the warders said – what exercise? 'We were able to quote chapter and verse from the rules that we were allowed one hour's exercise a day and we got it, but very reluctantly.' The next day all the other women insisted on their hour of exercise. It was November and the warders made them go out without their coats. There wasn't the same demand the following day but at least they had established their right.

The other women, many of them in jail for petty theft, begging and other minor crimes, couldn't understand why Máirín and Marie McMahon had risked going to jail for something like a political demonstration. 'Try explaining that to some poor sod who is in there because she hasn't a ha'penny, who has never had any money … It got to the point where I would do a lot *not* to explain what I was in there for.'[224]

In an interview with *The Sunday World,* a few years after her ordeal, Máirín still had vivid recollections of her time in Mountjoy. *'It's the crying I remember most'* was the headline as she recalled "Grown women crying hopelessly, sobbing like babies"[225] when they were locked into their cells at 7.30pm for the night.

Máirín remembered the endless monotony, long days with little to do. She recalled "Sometimes I would

---

224 *Stopper, ch. 2*
225 *Sunday World,* 6th January 1974

start rows to break the boredom, but no one would row with me." It was a litany of horrors – starchy food, broken heating, no pens to write with and the indignity of 'slopping out' (there were no in-cell toilets and prisoners had to queue to empty their chamber pots each morning). It is no wonder that for six months after she left prison Máirín was 'completely withdrawn and if anyone mentioned prison she would 'go into hysterics'[226]

Newspaper headline recounting Máirín's difficult experience in prison.

---

226 *Ibid,*

Sometimes rules were made up on the spot, such as stopping the women from singing although there was no official rule against it. Máirín thought that if you can find it in your heart to sing you should be encouraged. The women worked during the day on sewing machines and hemming sheets. In the evening they played Scrabble but the warders wouldn't give them a pen to keep the score. To make it interesting the women sometimes played without the E and A letters.

Prison Improvements

After her release Máirín spoke to her friend and *Irish Times* journalist, Mary Maher, about her ordeal and how complaints were dealt with. While in jail Máirín had told a member of the visiting committee, a supposedly independent group of people who visited prisons and reported annually to the Department of Justice, that the heating had been broken for three weeks. In response she was told by the warmly dressed woman that the cells "are as warm as my sitting room." Another prisoner was informed that "you get lovely food here, better than you would in your own homes."[227] Máirín and Marie McMahon, probably because they were assertive and 'educated', were allowed some privileges - to have an extra bath or knit in their cells - that the other women didn't get.

---

227 *The Irish Times*, 28th January 1972

Maher wrote a series of articles for *The Irish Times* about the women's prison which provoked a lot of public debate, including within the Dáil. As a result, when Máirín was briefly back in jail less than a year later, there were improvements. The food served now had a touch of Vitamin C Máirín noted, "a whole tomato sliced up with the evening bread and cheese.... and there were three slivers of cheese instead of two... and from all reports I'm told they sometimes have scrambled eggs on toast."[228] After Máirín's demand for exercise, it was now commonplace for all women prisoners to be allowed daily exercise. As she put it, "There is still nothing to do but at least everyone can go out in the fresh air and walk around for an hour."[229] Other improvements included the table tennis table having a net and some bats and balls. Small,inch by inch gains they certainly were.

War Ending

Whatever else prison does for its occupants there is plenty of time to think. Again, Máirín used the time well. On a previous jail sojourn, she decided to pursue the women's liberation issue. On this visit she decided she wanted to do something to highlight the awfulness of the prison system.

In May 1975 the war in Vietnam came to an end. *The Irish Times* reported that "National Liberation

228 *The Irish Times*, 18th October 1972
229 ibid

Front troops rolled into the South Vietnamese capitol (Saigon) yesterday virtually unopposed, to the great relief of the population which had feared a bloody last-minute battle."[230] It was one of the bloodiest conflicts in the second half of the twentieth century with many thousands of lives needlessly lost. The Irish Voice on Vietnam said the outcome "was a lesson for people everywhere that if they had a good cause, courage and leadership to unite the vast majority, nothing would defeat them."[231]

And Máirín had the satisfying memory of scoring a direct hit on the US President's car with her half dozen eggs.

---

230 *The Irish Times,* 1st May 1975
231 *Irish Press*, 1st May 1975

9. Back in Sinn Féin

Máirín was joint general secretary of Sinn Féin from 1969 to 1977, eight turbulent years. Along with housing, apartheid, Vietnam, prisoners and other issues, her main responsibility was to look after the day-to-day operation of the party.Most of the campaigns she was involved in became part of the job. Others had to be managed in her spare time, if she had any.

It was a hugely demanding workload which eventually proved impossible to maintain. One historian of that period reckoned that "Probably the most significant female leader that emerged from this period (1956-`1973) within the Southern political movement was Máirín De Burca."[232]

Despite her hugely demanding job Máirín made sure to make time for a social life. 'I was and am an opera buff and always found the money to go to the Dublin Grand Opera Society (DGOS) Spring and Autumn opera seasons. I remember going to my first opera in Dublin's Gaiety theatre, '*The Barber of Seville*.' I sent off a postal order for 5 shillings which was all I had. I got a ticket in the very back row right up top. I was enchanted.'

---

232 Tara Keenan Johnson, op cit., ch 5

Luckily for Máirín she had friends 'who had absolutely no interest in politics.' With them she could cycle out to the sea for a swim and then back to someone's flat for tea. 'I suppose you could say it was a nice, quiet lovely way to counter the almost constant political stuff which could be stressful to say the least.' And then there was always the safe harbour of home where she could put her feet up, read and relax.

Tony Heffernan

Back in head office Máirín was about to get a new work colleague. Sean O'Cionnaith became joint general secretary with Máirín when the party had the funds to employ two people. They got on well together, except for cleaning the office toilets. 'I said we would do a week on, week off. I did my week and when his turn came he said he didn't think they needed cleaning.' Máirín was not impressed.

O'Cionnaith eventually moved on to other work in the party and was replaced in August 1971 by twenty-two-year-old Tony Heffernan. Heffernan took up the job with some trepidation as he knew Máirín's reputation as a formidable figure in the party, with a track record of protests, arrests and court cases. For him Máirín was like a "coiled spring, carrying all the injustices of the world on her shoulders. I was very much the young boy coming in to work with this famous, legendary figure."[233] Máirín

233 Tony Heffernan interview

was a woman with definite views on many issues and was not afraid to challenge other people even when it was unpopular.

When Heffernan started working alongside Máirín some people told him, "you're a brave man...she could be grumpy, but she was also enormously charming when in good form."[234] And she needed to be at her charming best to deal with Heffernan's regular annoyance when she fried fish on the office Super Ser heater for the stray cats she often looked after. Máirín and cats got on very well together.

Shortly after he became joint general secretary Heffernan was quickly 'into battle' alongside Máirín. The issue this time was the detention of *United Irishman* editor Seamus O'Tuathail who was unfortunate to be in Belfast when internment was introduced in August 1971. In response Máirín and Tony decided to occupy the Department of Foreign Affairs in Dublin's St. Stephens Green. Máirín believed in the direct approach. 'We went to the Green but didn't see the big car down the road. We raced in and up to an office where we barricaded ourselves in. We were careful to say to the staff they were free to go as we were afraid of charges. One girl stayed and then left after about thirty minutes. We came out onto a balcony overlooking the Green and said hello to everyone.'

---

234 ibid

*Máirín and Bernadette Devlin, M.P. for Mid-Ulster, at an
anti-internment protest meeting outside Leinster House. 1970.
Photograph: Jack McManus/THE IRISH TIMES.*

'What we didn't know is that the British ambassador was
in the building at the time and behind his big car was
the Special Branch. I'm sure someone was transferred
to the Aran islands afterwards.' The protestors had the
honour of being some of the first to be charged under
The Forcible Entry and Occupation Act. They were fined
£2. Heffernan didn't pay and six months later a guard
arrived to his mother's door saying he would be arrested
if he didn't pay up. Mrs Heffernan obliged.[235]

---

235 Kenny, op. cit. ch. 3

Regular Protests

Protests such as these were grist to the mill for Máirín in those confrontational times. Tony Heffernan regards her as "one of the bravest persons I've met. At demos when trouble started, I would be gone like a light, Máirín would stand her ground and sometimes ended up with stitches in her head."[236]

The occupation of the Department of Foreign Affairs was a spontaneous event and Máirín didn't bother seeking approval from the party hierarchy. In a similar vein she rushed into the Sinn Féin office one day and told Heffernan that the British Ambassador's car was parked outside Dublin's Gresham Hotel. They both jumped on to their motorbikes, raced to the Gresham and threw a tin of paint over the Ambassador's Rolls Royce before racing away. Working with Máirín was certainly never dull.[237]

Padraig Yeates also worked in the Sinn Féin office alongside Máirín and Heffernan. For him Máirín was a "highly articulate woman, in your face. She was always organising protests against evictions, and you would be press ganged into joining in. She was a tearaway and for us she seemed totally unintimidatable, a force of nature."[238] Like Jack Charlton, Máirín had no problem in putting her colleagues 'under pressure' when she needed them to do something.

---

236 Tony Heffernan interview
237 ibid
238 Padraig Yeates Interview

Yeates was conscious also of the way Máirín separated her work from the rest of her life. "When she got on that scooter and went home she was gone. She kept her private life and her activism quite separate, whereas for most of us if you weren't in the office, you were in the pub, at a picket or selling papers."[239]

Away from it all. Máirín at home in her Ballsbridge flat c.1972. De Burca archive.

---

239 ibid

Despite all the conflict in the North, Sinn Féin 'down South' continued with its leftward and radical approach to social issues. 'Sit ins' and even 'fish ins' became a regular occurrence. Part of the thinking behind 'fish ins' was to develop the party's support in rural Ireland. A stretch of the river Blackwater in Lismore was the focus of one protest in 1972. That particular stretch was owned by the Duke of Devonshire and was ripe for action. Máirín, along with Tony Heffernan and Sean O'Cionnaith, came from Dublin to protest. Heffernan dramatically declared on the riverbank "that the struggle in Lismore was the same as the struggle being waged by the people in the North. The protestors, with the Gardaí and Special Branch looking on, then proceeded to cast their lines but no salmon were caught." 'A Fish in Without Fish' ran one newspaper headline.[240]

On another occasion a large house and estate in Kerry was up for auction in Dublin. As the auctioneer asked for bids Máirín stood up and said that "the proceedings were illegal, and nobody had a right to sell the property of the Irish people. On behalf of (Official) Sinn Féin whoever buys it will never be allowed to enjoy it."[241] After that not so subtle warning the auction was cancelled and Sinn Féin's support in Kerry grew. By the middle of 1971, the party in the county had enough members to set up a second cumann.[242]

---

240 Corkman, 22nd April 1972
241 The Irish Times, 7th July 1971
242 Hanley and Miller, ch 7

The party's pamphlet *Stolen Waters* was one of their most popular publications. Speaking at another 'fish in' in Donegal Máirín said there was a link between "the fishermen of Inver, the cement strikers of Drogheda and Limerick and the oppressed of the Falls and Bogside."[243] It was dramatic stuff, and it helped the party develop outside of the cities.

Ground Rents

Back in the capital Sinn Féin continued to focus on the housing issue. By the mid-1970s the housing action committee was gone but the protests and the attempts to stop evictions continued. The party was seen as the 'go to' organisation for anyone with a 'notice to quit' and Máirín enjoyed one particular success. 'The city sheriff was there to evict, we were there to protest and a Garda inspector and a couple of guards were there as well. The sheriff quite abruptly said to the Inspector – 'clear these people', and the Inspector turned to him and said, 'clear them yourself' and walked off'. A rare but enjoyable victory.

The inequities of the ground rent system was another housing issue that Máirín and Sinn Féin fought against vigorously during the 1970s. Ground rents were and are a system where an annual rent is paid to a landlord who own the freehold to a property. So, even though someone might 'own' a house, the ground it is built on is owned by someone else and sometimes that owner was

---

243 ibid

184

a British landowner, in effect an absentee landlord. Not surprisingly, ground rents were hugely unpopular and Sinn Féin campaigned regularly on the issue.

In their detailed pamphlet *Ground Rent is Robbery* Sinn Féin described ground rent as "immoral and its abolition is long overdue." In dramatic, fighting language they wrote that "As Irish people it behoves us to rid ourselves of this black rent of history and apply the principles established by the Land League." The party saw it as "the smashing of the link with the conquest."[244]

Front cover of Official Sinn Fein's pamphlet on the ground rents issue. 1974. Tony Heffernan archive, UCD archives.

244 Official Sinn Féin – *Ground Rent is Robbery* (Repsol Publications, *1974*)

Máirín was not alone in her opposition to this unjust rent. Protests were led by the Association of Combined Residents Association (ACRA) and other groups. Indeed, a campaign against ground rents organised by ACRA was launched at an event in Ennis, County Clare, organised by Sinn Féin.

It wasn't long, however, before there was conflict. ACRA had a policy in place that they would share a public platform on the issue with other groups who had similar aims. By September 1973 that approach had changed, and they accused Sinn Féin of being "more of a hindrance than a help" and called on Máirín to "get off our backs." Máirín responded by pointing out that Sinn Féin had been campaigning on the issue for four years and ACRA was now trying to become "a respectable body".[245] And 'respectable' was one of the last things Máirín wanted to be.

ACRA was motivated by its desire not to be associated with any political party. The fact that they made it a personal criticism of Máirín did not help. Despite this disagreement, and after years of campaigning, a Landlord and Tenant (Ground Rents) Act came into force in 1978. It prevented landlords from creating any new ground rents and introduced a system whereby people still paying ground rents could 'buy out' their landlord. It was an important victory against a much-disliked system and Máirín and Sinn Féin had played an important role in it.

---

245 *Dublin Post*, 5th September 1973

Europe

Apart from national issues Sinn Féin also looked outward. The plan in 1973 for Ireland to join the European Economic Community (EEC), as it was then called, was opposed by the party. There were protests in Dublin city and at the airport when Foreign Minister Paddy Hillery flew to Brussels to sign Ireland up for membership. In her own inimitable manner Máirín protested by painting a slogan on a telephone kiosk in Dublin's Lower Abbey Street. When she inevitably appeared in court, she replied to the charges by saying "she believed that membership of the EEC would finally alienate the Irish people and she thought it was more important to warn them of it than to mark the back of a telephone box."[246] Strange logic, but perhaps the innocent phone box contained an important message for the public?

Máirín was regularly on the streets about the issue, leafleting, sloganeering and putting up anti-EEC posters. This 'littering' drew upon her the anger of one of Dublin's free sheet papers which Máirín rebutted by pointing out that she objected to "huge wall hoardings telling me that Smirnoff turns somebody on and TV ads showing some woman having orgasms using some bloody washing powder or other."[247] When it came to the poll on joining the EEC, the Irish electorate were unimpressed by Official Sinn Féin's policy and voted to join by a huge majority.

---

246 *Irish Independent*, 13th April 1973
247 *Dublin Post*, 21st January 1972

Máirín on her Vespa scooter with an anti-EEC slogan on its front.
1973. De Burca archive.

General Election

As part of its engagement in democratic politics Official
Sinn Féin put forward ten candidates in the 1973 general

election. It was the first time the party had contested a general election in the South since 1961. Máirín was the candidate in Dublin's North Central constituency and campaigned on a radical programme. She called for the declaration of a housing emergency and an end to speculation in building land.[248] The party's overall campaign slogan was 'People before Profit' (they really should have copyrighted that phrase).

In her election leaflet it was noted that Máirín was aged 35, single and a native of Newbridge. She emphasised also that "if our candidates are elected, **they will take their seats in Leinster House** (Máirín's emphasis)."[249] The era of abstention was well and truly over.

However, campaigning and canvassing wasn't something Máirín enjoyed. 'I did well on first preferences, but I didn't get transfers from the other parties. We had good fun and a bit of craic with people on the canvass… but I'm not good at knocking on doors and I'm not good at glad handing and being nice to people. Sometimes I couldn't face being nice to another human being. I would have to go home and take a couple of aspirins.'

Máirín campaigned on the issues she had advocated on throughout her career - housing, poverty and discrimination. During her campaign she said it was her intention "to continue the battle started in 1967 by Sinn

248 *Irish Examiner*, 13th February 1973
249 Máirín De Burca, Election Leaflet, 1973, De Burca archive

Féin and the Dublin Housing Action Committee for decent homes, no matter what Government is returned in this election."[250]

Dublin North Central

Maureen De Burca is aged 35 and is joint General Secretary for Sinn Fein. She is single and is a native of Droichíd Nua. Co. Kildare. She was founded member of the Dublin Housing Action Committee and the Irish Womens Liberation Movement. Miss De Burca is well known for her activities on behalf of the homeless people of Dublin.

VOTE NO. I
Maırín
De BURCA
SINN FÉIN

Máirín's election leaflet for the 1973 general election.
De Burca archive.

250 *Irish Examiner*, 16th February 1973

Máirín was up against some heavyweight politicians, such as Fianna Fail's George Colley, Labour's Michael O' Leary and Fine Gael's Luke Belton. In the end she got 1,667 first preferences but was never in with a chance of taking a seat. Máirín has no regrets about not being elected. 'It would have been an unhappy few years and then they would be relying on you to keep your seat. Other people made it and were good at it and well done to them, but it wouldn't have been me.'

It was a very disappointing election for Official Sinn Féin. Their twelve candidates got a combined total of 15,000 first preference votes. None got anywhere near to being elected with well-established Seamus Costello coming second last in Wicklow. Tony Heffernan recalls the naivety of the party at that time. "We had no one with prior experience in our constituency. We didn't even know about things like getting the electoral register."[251]

After their poor performance, the party engaged in a detailed exercise in internal navel gazing. Various scenarios for the party of the future were suggested, including one for the 'model of a revolutionary party.' There were also proposals to turn Official Sinn Féin into "a Marxist party run on Leninist principles."[252] Given the situation in the North and the many social problems in the South it sounded like a version of Nero fiddling while Rome burns.

---

251 Kenny, op.cit ch 4
252 Hanley and Miller, ch.7

Business as Usual

Máirín distanced herself from too much internal agonising and after the election it was business as usual. During the rest of 1973 she fought against the proposed use of the Forcible Entry Act to evict squatters and objected to an Irish Life planning application to knock down houses in Northumberland Square, off Dublin's Abbey St, and build a large office block in their place.[253] Ironically, these houses had been given, on a temporary basis, to the Dublin Simon Community to house homeless people. When Irish Life got their planning permission the Simon residents, despite some protests, had to move on.

In December 1973 Máirín launched a scathing attack on the Catholic church's attitude to contraception. Speaking at a meeting in Trinity College she described the church's approach as "a deliberate and disgusting attempt to stampede the members of the legislature and instil feelings of guilt into couples using contraception." It was a no holds barred attack and she went on to say that while it was not considered alright to 'kill' a 10-week-old foetus "it was quite acceptable to burn children with napalm so long as it was in the anti-communist cause."[254] For the Ireland of the 1970s this type of attack was rare and certainly wouldn't have endeared Máirín to at least some of the electorate in her constituency.

---

253 *Irish Press*, 17th October 1973
254 *Irish Press*, 1st December 1973

Local Election

Despite her reservations about campaigning, Máirín agreed to run in the 1974 local elections. Sinn Féin's campaigns on housing and ground rents resonated with the public and Máirín received 974 votes, 6.6% of the total. However, it wasn't enough, and she missed out again. Nationally Official Sinn Féin won six seats, just beaten by Provisional Sinn Féin who managed seven.

Despite not getting elected in 1973 and 1974 the pump was primed for another left-wing politician, former Sinn Féin member Tony Gregory, to become a TD some years later. Máirín is clear about that contribution; 'It should be understood that the activities we engaged in across the Dublin North Central constituency enabled Tony Gregory to be elected as a TD (Gregory was first elected in 1982). There is no doubt about that in my mind.'

What is noticeable about Máirín's political activity in the first few years of the 1970s is what isn't there. Yes, there are all 'her issues' which she campaigned on relentlessly, but little mention of what was happening in the North, apart from her occasional condemnation of IRA violence. She did take part in various debates on the issue, but it was almost as if events North and South were happening in parallel worlds. Given her position in Sinn Féin, 'the Troubles' had to be part of her work, but in terms of time devoted to the North and public pronouncements there was little to see or hear. Instead, she continued to focus her attention on more immediate day to day struggles, one of which was her fraught relationship with the guards and the legal system.

TRINITY HISTORICAL SOCIETY DEBATE: Máirín and Eamonn McCann apparently keeping their own counsel while Mr. Constantine Fitzgibbon speaks to Lord Brookeborough during the Historical Society debate in Trinity College. MOTION: "this house should get tough on terrorists." The motion was lost. Photograph and caption: Pat Langan/THE IRISH TIMES.

10. Taking On The Legal System

Máirín liked to ' keep her hand in' with various protests, rows with the Gardaí and appearances in court. Her array of dealings with the forces of law and order was wide ranging and impressive.

In May 1971 her former IWLM colleague, Nell McCafferty, reported in *The Irish Times* that Máirín had appeared before the courts seventeen times in the previous three years. McCafferty went through the appearances in detail - burning the Union Jack, participating in a sit in, protests about the jailing of squatters, the protest in the Pro Cathedral in front of President De Valera. They were all listed including the time she helpfully told the court she had broken a window in the German Cultural Institute by mistake as she thought it was the British Embassy.[255] She got a £5 pound fine for that one, and maybe a reduction for honesty?

In 1972 Máirín was again fined £5 for spraying a slogan on a telephone box and ordered to pay 50p compensation.[256] In the same year she was convicted, along with many others, for 'watching and besetting' the

---

255 Nell McCafferty – *Women in Court 3 – The Irish Times,* 4th May 1971
256 *The Irish Times,* 21st April 1972

home of Taoiseach Jack Lynch.[257] Prior to that Máirín had picketed the Taoiseach's home protesting against the suspected introduction of internment in the South (which never happened). Marin explained to reporters, "It was a nice summer evening and we decided to do something."[258] She was being ironic, but there was an element of truth in what she said. Picketing and protesting is what Máirín did for 'entertainment'.

The following year she was fined £2 for using threatening and insulting behaviour. She was seen by a guard giving out leaflets to passing cars and when a driver refused one she shoved it into his windscreen wiper, whereupon the driver got out of his car and a tussle ensued.[259] If reported accurately, it was an unseemly incident and not one of Máirín's finest hours. It is hard not to get the impression that this form of protest was almost compulsive. A style of action that was always readily, and maybe too readily, used.

Máirín appeared in all the courts, from the District Court to the High and Supreme Courts and back down again. She was convicted a number of times but also won some important cases. Apart from her win over the Juries Act, she also had her victory in the Supreme Court over her committal to jail for contempt - this was the case where she refused to divulge the names of squatters in a Dublin house. She also had that distinction of having

257 *Irish Press*, 6th January 1973
258 *The Irish Times*, 17th July 1971
259 *Evening Herald*, 6th January 1973

her case mentioned in three courts - District, High and Supreme Courts - on the same day.[260] The newspapers of the time are full of reports of Máirín variously being fined, remanded, sentenced, released and sent to prison. The judges must have dreaded seeing this diminutive but determined figure entering their courts.

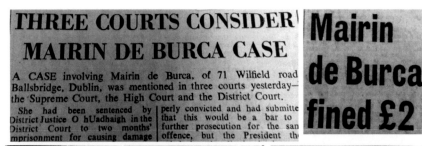

THREE COURTS CONSIDER MAIRIN DE BURCA CASE

A CASE involving Mairin de Burca, of 71 Wilfield road Ballsbridge, Dublin, was mentioned in three courts yesterday— the Supreme Court, the High Court and the District Court.

She had been sentenced by District Justice O hUadhaigh in the District Court to two months' imprisonment for causing damage | perly convicted and had submitte that this would be a bar to further prosecution for the san offence, but the President th

Mairin de Burca fined £2

MAIRIN DE BURCA SENT TO JAIL

Refuses to disclose names

THE PRESIDENT of the High Court, Mr. Justice O'Keeffe yesterday ordered that Miss Mairin de Burca, Wilfield road Ballsbridge, Dublin, be committed to Mountjoy prison fo contempt for refusing to answer a question put to her by th judge. She was taken from court by two gardai.

She refused to tell the judge the names of families occupying a house at 34 Upper Gardiner street, | being advised as to the consequence of her action, did not wish change her attitude. Subsequentl

Mairin de Burca fined £5 for damaging kiosk

Mairin de Burca, of Wilfield Road, Ballsbridge, was fined £5 and ordered to pay 50p compensation in the Dublin District Court on Wednesday, when convicted of damaging a telephone kiosk in Lower Abbey Street, Dublin, on

Press reports of some of Máirín's many court appearances. Early 1970s. De Burca archive.

Fearless Woman

Because of her constant interaction with the courts Máirín had no fear of them and saw the legal system as something to be used. As she explained in an interview in 1973, "I am using the law against itself. I want it to be

---

260 *Irish Independent*, 18th June 1971

seen and proved that people do have the right to protest against what they consider to be injustice; that they need not fear the remote anonymous control of their lives which they see embodied in the magisterial trappings of the law and the system."

It was a calculated approach where Máirín believed strongly that "The law as presently constituted and enforced is unjust and I break the law, test it in court, to show that it is so."[261] She would have been a brilliant barrister.

Máirín's many protests and court appearances inevitably led her into frequent contact with the guards. To say there was a mutual suspicion would be putting it mildly. That attitude went all the way back to her childhood. In an article she wrote for *The Irish Times,* Máirín recalled that "When I was a child living in Chicago, I was afraid of three types of people, policemen, blacks and drunks."[262]

That early fear was compounded by her real-life experiences as an adult. In the same article she wrote that, "I and my comrades have known what it is like to be attacked by a party of guards, dressed in riot gear, armed with iron bars, wooden staves and batons, being beaten down three flights of stairs, dumped into a hospital to be patched up before being brought back to spend the night in the Bridewell (Garda station). I have a phobia

---

261 ibid
262 *The Irish Times*, 10th January 1973

of staircases for life after being thrown down steps twice in my life, once by a member of the Special Branch and once by a uniformed Guard."[263]

Máirín was present in Merrion Square when the British Embassy was burned down in February 1972 after 'Bloody Sunday' in Derry. She recalls that six guards "came over to us and started beating us down Merrion Square. My head was cracked open, my face was smashed against the railings and my friend was also beaten but not injured." Máirín received one final blow and the guard told her to find an ambulance and get to hospital.[264]

Consistent Critic

It is not surprising, therefore, that Máirín was a consistent critic of the guards throughout her political life. A week after Máirín's article was published, *The Irish Times* ran an interview with two anonymous guards, called Garda A and Garda B. Commenting on a protest at the British Embassy, where Máirín claimed she was beaten, Garda A said, "If Miss De Burca was beaten at the Embassy, she must have deserved it."[265]

Garda B criticised the idea of the "defenceless poor demonstrator...I've seen them... coming toward us with bottles, bars, slivers of glass. One fellow even attacked an

---

263   Ibid.
264 *The Irish Times,* 10th January 1973
265 *The Irish Times,* 17th January 1973

Inspector on one occasion with a pike."[266] The same guard went on to describe his experience of standing in front of demonstrators and being spat upon and subjected to foul abuse. He pointed out that many protests were peaceful but often "Miss De Burca's people" break the law and have to be dealt with.

Garda A, sometimes the 'soft cop' of this duo, did acknowledge that excessive force was sometimes used. To which Garda B added that in the Dublin area no prisoner is ever beaten in the station but that it does happen occasionally "down the country."[267]

After pointing out that many guards were engaged in community and social work, both guards finished the interview with Garda A stating that he "wouldn't waste my time talking to Miss De Burca and her fellow protestors. They are professional agitators, and their prime enemy is the Garda Síochána." Garda B, while acknowledging Máirín's right to protest, said his job was "to ensure that in doing so she doesn't overstep the limits of the law. That doesn't mean we are against social justice or change."[268]

This article was a rare insight into the thinking of the 'ordinary guard' and the only pity was that the two guards were anonymous.

---

266 Ibid.
267 Ibid.
268 ibid

That anonymity was one of the many issues Máirín and some of her former IWLM colleagues went to town on in their responses to the interview. Máirín in her letter to the paper, took 'great exception' to the guards being allowed to speak without identifying themselves and then proceeded to challenge the Garda version of events at the various protests mentioned. It was predictable stuff and at times her letter reads like a therapy session where she offloads years of resentment. With some feeling she questions whether one of the guards feels he is doing his job "by beating me half unconscious? Is it also his job to arrest beggars, charge children, kick protestors if they disrupt traffic for half an hour?"[269]

The responses from women who were one step removed from the debate were probably more effective. Mrs. Gaj weighed into the debate and wrote about her own family experience. "To say that prisoners are never beaten up … is completely untrue. My son was beaten up on two occasions, once in the station and once on the way to the station. Despite the fact that he was examined by independent doctors, senior counsel more or less advised that it was a waste of time and energy trying to prosecute a Garda."[270]

Marie McMahon added her own personal story. Describing when she and others were arrested and saw a guard who "pushed (her colleague) against the wall and

---

269 Máirín De Burca Letter, *The Irish Times*, January 1973
270 Margaret Gaj Letter, *The Irish Times,* January 1973

hit him with his fist on the face several times." When she challenged this behaviour, she was told "that my friend deserved what he got. The next day the judge dismissed the case against Marie McMahon and her friend."[271]

Three separate accounts, albeit from radical women activists, did lend substance to the claim that guards were regularly mistreating people who protested.

Lack of Accountability

The Irish Times went so far as to write a long editorial on the subject. It considered one of the most disturbing aspects of the affair was the belief "that the average citizen has no comeback if he considers himself wronged by the police."[272] The editorial highlighted the lack of accountability of the Gardaí to the public and noted also a constant stream of complaints from prisons which the Minister for Justice refused to account for in the Dáil.

This whole episode did not yield instant results but Máirín and *The Irish Times* had brought into the public domain an important concern about the way the country's police force behaved and misbehaved. In a series of investigative articles in the late 1970s, the same newspaper wrote about the existence of a Garda 'Heavy Gang', who were reputed to extract confessions to various crimes by using oppressive and

---

271 Marie McMahon Letter, *The Irish Times*,9th January 1973
272 *The Irish Times*, 12th February 1973

abusive techniques. There were regular accusations in the courts about forced confessions and, because of 'the Troubles' in the North, suggestions that the normal rules did not apply within the force.

In 1977 Amnesty International published a report alleging ill-treatment of prisoners by Gardaí. It looked at 28 cases involving such allegations while the accused were in police custody. The ill treatment of prisoners was backed up by medical and other evidence. It found the names of certain Garda members appeared repeatedly in cases where they were dispatched from Dublin to serious crime investigations nationwide and where confessions were then secured. The abuses ranged from pushing and shoving to severe beatings, and food and water deprivation.

In an article she wrote in 1977 Máirín herself referred to a Garda 'Special Interrogation Squad' which had come from Dublin to interview suspects. Máirín reported that one of the suspects claimed he jumped out of the third-floor window of the Garda station in an apparent suicide bid. Another man was referred by his doctor for psychiatric treatment after he was released. Máirín also reported that in the same week as the accused men made these claims the Minister for Justice, Paddy Cooney, told newly qualified guards that they were not exempt from obeying the law.[273]

---

273 *The Irish People*, 11th February 1977

From the vantage point of 21st century Ireland this behaviour may seem surprising but in the Ireland of the 1970s and 'the Troubles' none of this was unusual. Eventually, after many years of lobbying and campaigning, reforms with regard to the accountability of Gardaí came into being. It wasn't until 2007 that the Garda Ombudsman's office was set up. It took a very long time and many suspects and accused undoubtedly suffered in the meantime. However, the persistence and determination of Máirín De Burca and others did eventually contribute to much needed reform.

11. The Purists' Party

Right through the 1970s, while 'the Troubles' raged in the North, Official Sinn Féin was beset by internal controversy. It seemed almost compulsory for left wing parties to become embroiled in disagreement as to how to achieve socialist nirvana. There were those in the 'green corner', such as Seamus Costello, who, despite earlier declarations about mass agitation, prioritised the national struggle and the use of the gun if necessary. And then there were those in the 'red corner' who wanted to focus on the working-class fight for freedom. People in that camp referred to their opponents as 'right wing militarist Costello-ites'.[274]

While Máirín was certainly in the 'red corner', she tried to avoid getting bogged down with ideological debates. However, she continued to speak out against the use of physical force and in a speech to students in Trinity College in 1974 she said "I now believe the Provisional IRA are terrorists and the activities of the present IRA campaign bear no resemblance to the IRA activities of the 20s, 30, 40s and 50s."[275]

---

274 Hanley and Miller, ch.7
275 *Irish Independent*, 24th October 1974

The distinction between the IRA past and present could be seen as an attempt by Máirín to justify her support for the IRA border campaign of the 1950s. Notwithstanding that, it was a speech full of real feeling where she went on to declare that "There is nothing particularly revolutionary in killing innocent people. There is nothing radical in blowing up a factory employing several hundred people and claiming that you have struck a mighty blow against capitalism."[276]

Party Induction

Those in the 'red corner' in Official Sinn Féin, such as Sean Garland, Eoin Ó Murchú and Eoghan Harris, wanted to pursue a definite socialist agenda with Garland keen on the idea of creating a revolutionary party. Official Sinn Féin began to take itself very seriously as they sought the workers' revolution. All new members were told they had to "complete a probationary period of 6 months before they may become full members. All new members must complete a series of 6 lectures covering various aspects of Movement Policy, Objectives, Strategy and History."[277]

This induction wasn't for the faint hearted but the aim was to have new members who were 'ideologically pure' when their probation was complete. A discussion document on organisational structure included a

276 Ibid.
277 *Sinn Féin New Members Handbook* (no date), Tony Heffernan Archive, UCD Archives.

proposal on the *'Evolution from 6 years old, within the Movement and the Young Revolutionary Movement'*. The idea was that children could join Fianna Eireann from age 6 and learn 'History and Scouting'. And from there, when aged 14, they could graduate to the 'Young Revolutionary Movement'.[278] It seemed extraordinary that no one held a hand up and said 'Stop this Nonsense'.

Education of party members was seen as an ongoing priority and a house the party had acquired in Mornington, County Louth was the venue for various education programmes. Máirín was not a 'pupil' in the 'Mornington school' but did attend a series of lectures in Dublin with mixed results. 'They were interesting enough with a Q and A at the end. The only one who didn't allow a Q and A after his lecture was Eoghan Harris. When he finished, he walked off the stage and you weren't allowed ask a question.'

Lecture series such as these were taken very seriously by some. 'It was suggested we sit an exam at the end of the series. You had really good members worried what would happen if you didn't pass. I raised it at an Árd Comhairle meeting and I got Tomás MacGiollas backing so it didn't run. An examination, come on!'

Máirín's colleague Padraig Yeates recalls that some of the education courses would start with a full house but

278 Sinn Féin, *Discussion Document on Organisation and Structure*, August 1973, Tony Heffernan Archive, UCD Archives

by the end there might only be a handful of people left. Yeates, however, found the Mornington school to be quite worthwhile and it did discourage participants from going over to the Provos. Despite his support for these education courses Yeates himself was not immune from criticism within the party. At one point an attempt was made to court martial him for 'Trotskyist tendencies', but that came to nothing.[279]

Flashpoint

When the 1973 Árd Feis came round debate between 'green' and 'red' was an almost inevitable flashpoint. Seamus Costello strongly opposed a motion on potential support for a reformed police force in the North and it was defeated. However, a motion seeking to emphasise the primacy of the national struggle was also defeated.

At times internal politics went to farcical lengths. The party had been involved in the 'Resources Protection Campaign' (RPC) which aimed to highlight the need for the State to protect the country's oil, gas and coal reserves. For some reason the members involved in the RPC didn't want the group open to the wider party membership. Máirín heard one day about an upcoming meeting and with some annoyance prepared a large poster advertising the event. At the last minute the venue was changed so 'ordinary' members couldn't attend. So much for a united struggle.

---

279 Padraig Yeates interview

Debate on these ideological issues spread to the party branches. On one occasion the Ballymun branch engaged in a detailed discussion on the 'Two Nations' theory, a theory that suggested there were separate Protestant/ Loyalist and Catholic/Nationalist 'nations' on the island which needed to be accommodated. A frustrated Proinsias De Rossa suggested that they suspend the meeting and go and knock on the doors of the flats in Ballymun and ask people what they thought of the 'Two Nations' theory. Silence and end of discussion. And De Rossa soon moved to another branch of the party.[280]

The party continued its leftward move with various discussion documents being produced as to the way forward. How to create the 'revolutionary party' was an ongoing focus of debate and, on one occasion, Sean Garland submitted a discussion paper on 'The Organisation of the Proletariat's Armed Forces'.[281] It was all so deadly serious and, looking back, somewhat ridiculous.

Within this environment there was intense debate, rows and threats. Eventually there was a move against Seamus Costello, and he was expelled from the Official IRA in 1974 and then came under scrutiny within the party itself. An internal report, prepared by Máirín and Tony Heffernan, found that Costello had rigged voting at an Árd Fheis and organised 'block voting' for membership

280 Proinsias De Rossa interview
281 Hanley and Millar, ch. 7

of the Árd Comhairle. It wasn't a hanging offence, but Costello was suspended for an initial six month period and a full enquiry was arranged.[282]

Despite being out of Official Sinn Féin, Costello, against the wishes of the party, continued to attend meetings of Wicklow County Council where he was an elected councillor and ran in the 1974 local elections as an 'Independent Sinn Féin' candidate. He was elected both to the Urban District Council and the County Council.

Despite these successes, Costello's days as a member of the party were numbered. He was called before another internal enquiry with Máirín one of those to pass judgement. 'I said to him - Seamus you and I go back a long way and there is no way my mind is made up. I want to hear what you have to say. He did make a statement, but I felt sorry I couldn't vote for him.' Costello was expelled from the party and members of the Official IRA were told not to have anything to do with him.[283]

Costello's departure was difficult for Máirín as she had known him since she was a sixteen-year-old girl in Bray. 'Seamus never accepted the move away from the gun... the one failing he had was his dedication to the gun.... Poor Seamus. He was in a minority. Most rational members realised the gun wasn't the way to go and it was harking back to old times.'

---

282 *Report to Sinn Féin Árd Comhairle*, 9th May 1974, Tony Heffernan Archive, UCD Archives
283 Hanley and Millar, ch. 7

IRSP

After his expulsion Costello and his colleagues formed the Irish Republican Socialist Party (IRSP) and its sister military wing the Irish National Liberation Army (INLA). It was a tense time for Máirín and her colleagues in Official Sinn Féin as there was a genuine fear of retribution. On one occasion Máirín cancelled a speech she was to give to students in University College Galway because of the 'present political circumstances.' Senior party figure, Sean Garland, was shot on his way home in Ballymun and there was talk of reprisals against the IRSP.[284]

Seamus Costello, Máirín's friend and former colleague, murdered in 1977.

Máirín had to watch her step. 'I was careful when I answered the door …. But I always felt Seamus wouldn't shoot me. They blamed me for the move against the gun

284 *Irish Independent*, 4th March 1975

and I did start it to an extent. Tomás Mac Giolla wrote to me later saying that I was responsible for the party's move away from the gun.' Costello continued his engagement with electoral politics but got less than 1,000 votes in the 1977 general election. Later that year he was shot dead sitting in his car in Dublin's inner city but the reason for this or who his killer was never came to light.

Sustained Assault

It wasn't just Máirín or her colleagues in the South who needed to be careful. In October 1975 a dispute between the Provisional IRA and the Official IRA led to a sustained assault on the Officials across Belfast. Over sixteen days there were one hundred armed attacks leading to eleven deaths.[285] Official Sinn Féin weren't too far off the mark in calling it a pogrom.

The following month Máirín and Tony Heffernan issued a public appeal asking people to "take a public stand on this matter and/or use whatever influence you may have with members or supporters of the Provisionals to have this murderous campaign ended."[286] With the help of local clergymen a truce was called but the scars ran deep, and tensions remained for a long time. The following year, speaking at Bodenstown, Máirín was typically uncompromising in her assessment. "The Catholic nationalist xenophobes were going to do to us what

---

285 Hanley and Millar, op. cit, ch 9
286 *De Burca and Heffernan letter*, 6th November 1975, Tony Heffernan archive, UCD Archives

they plan to do with one million of our Protestant fellow countrymen. But we survived."[287]

The political situation was extremely volatile, North and South, at this time. Anyone who was involved in the 'national struggle' had to be careful about what they said and where they said it. In spite of her anxiety about both the INLA and the Provisional IRA, Máirín was fearless in her continued criticism of the Provos. On the sixtieth anniversary of the 1916 Easter Rising, she addressed a commemoration event in Lurgan, County Armagh where she said that the IRA's "murderous campaign bore no relationship to the ideals of the men of 1916." She noted that the 1916 leaders surrendered to prevent further loss of life and asked, "By what possible perversion of the word Republican do our latter-day murderers claim kinship with such high minded but practical patriotism?"[288]

Sinn Féin and Women

Despite the ongoing violence in the North, 'down South' Official Sinn Féin continued its tortuous internal debates on the best ways to advance the socialist cause. Máirín preferred to focus on the day-to-day struggles of housing, welfare rights and women's rights. She worked hard to get women's issues on the agenda in the party. In October 1971 she succeeded in getting a resolution on equal pay,

---

287 Hanley and Millar, op cit, ch.9
288 *Irish People*, 20th April 1976

the availability of contraceptives and of divorce passed at that year's Árd Fheis.[289] It was a small but important step.

Sometimes, however, she couldn't avoid being dragged into internal debate. At one point the party's own paper *The Irish People* published an article which claimed that feminism was downgrading the class struggle. Máirín was angry and responded by labelling the attack 'the usual Trotskyite bullshit'. She pointed out that the class struggle was of little use to a woman who had experienced domestic abuse.[290]

In an internal party document she continued to challenge certain 'left wing' attitudes to women. She wrote "Somehow the notion has got around that so long as we join a trade union… and know roughly what Marx and Engels had to say about women, then that should be the full sum of our involvement with and interest in the subject of our own oppression." With regard to Marx, she pointedly noted that many women were "slightly unimpressed by a man who was not willing to put his words into practice with his own wife and whose family life was pretty appalling."[291] While Máirín may have been addressing women in this paper, there is no doubt she was looking over her shoulder at the Marxist purists who were trying to take over her party.

---

289 Tara Keenan Johnson, ibid, ch 5

290 ibid

291 Máirín De Burca, *Women and the Revolutionary Movement* (no date), De Burca archive

Although sometimes a minority voice in Official Sinn Féin, Máirín highlighted discrimination against women whenever she could. In 1973 she bluntly asserted that "There was hardly an organisation in the State which did not contribute to the exploitation, discrimination and, in many cases, degradation of women."[292] Máirín's long list of organisations referred to included Government, the Churches, trade unions, the Irish Housewives Association and the Irish Countrywomen's Association (ICA). With regard to the ICA,while acknowledging their positive work for rural women, she asked "Have they tried to politicise their members? Have they tried to encourage them to analyse their situation and to pull themselves out of it?"[293] This was strong stuff in 1970s Ireland but when Máirín De Burca was in full flow no one and nobody was safe and that included her colleagues in Sinn Féin.

Policy Document

In 1975 Official Sinn Féin published its first policy document on women, entitled *The Rights of Women in Ireland*. The following year the party's Árd Fheis debated a motion on equal pay for women but ignored the other difficulties women experienced such as proper access to contraception, health and childcare services. Máirín argued that such services would benefit workers as well as middle class women.

---

292 *The Irish Times*, 26th April 1973
293 ibid

By 1976 the party had established what it rather grandly called 'The National Women's Committee of Official Sinn Féin'. On March 9th that year, just after International Women's Day, the Committee picketed the Department of Justice in Dublin protesting against "all legislation which discriminates against women." Máirín, as their spokesperson, said that the gains women had made were "pathetically inadequate in comparison with remaining inequities."

Among the long list of inequalities referred to, Sinn Féin highlighted the marriage ban in public sector employment, the low paid jobs women were often stuck in and the lack of family planning and divorce. Máirín challenged newspapers who she believed treated women like 'imbeciles' and criticised *Hibernia* magazine (which she was to work for a few years later) for describing a Fianna Fail politician as 'sexy Sile De Valera'.[294]

American Tour

It was second time lucky for Máirín in her attempt to conduct a lecture tour of the United States. It was 1976 and things had changed. President Nixon had resigned in disgrace after the Watergate scandal and the war in Vietnam was over. Máirín's parents were naturalised US citizens and that helped her get a visa. She embarked on a speaking tour of several cities from the east to the

---

294 *The Irish Times*, 10th January 1976

west coast. Multiple lectures were given in various states on diverse issues such *'Irish Women's Rights'* and *'What is happening in Ireland Now?'* Despite the changes in the political climate, the FBI were still on her case. They doggedly recorded Máirín's visits to Boston, Chicago, Milwaukee, Minneapolis, New York, San Francisco, and many other locations.

Poster advertising Máirín's American lecture tour in 1976.
De Burca archive.

The level of attention and resources put into pursuing Máirín were extraordinary and many of her speeches, sometimes to just forty or fifty people, were attended by FBI personnel or their informants. How they disguised themselves is unknown although Máirín's FBI file notes that agents were scared to go to Berkeley University (scene of many student protests) in California where they wanted to serve some papers for Máirín to sign. These required her to register under the Foreign Agents Registration Act as she may have been raising funds for Sinn Féin.[295] In all likelihood it was another effort to intimidate Máirín and make clear to her she was being watched.

The FBI eventually approached Máirín with these papers at another event in a Californian university and were strongly criticised for impinging on academic independence and freedom of discussion. The Bureau defended its approach and their San Francisco office reported that "Agents' morale is greatly bolstered by the Bureau's firm stand to defend their exemplary performance of an extremely delicate assignment in a hostile environment ... (the serving of forms) to the Subject at a public gathering sponsored by Maoists and members of ... a communist oriented group."[296] So it was hats off to the FBI.

Máirín took the papers and said she would return them in ten days as requested. She was, however, one step

295 Máirín De Burca FBI File, De Burca archive
296 ibid

ahead of the Bureau. 'To delay the hearing, I took an explanatory booklet that came with the papers, picked a section at random and replied that under that section I was 'not guilty'. I knew being American they would seriously examine my claim and that would give me time to get home. It worked perfectly and I was back home before they could do anything. But I bet, being America, that charge is still there, and I would probably be arrested if I went back'.

In her lectures Máirín covered the position of women in Ireland and the overall political situation, both North and South. Some of the records made by the FBI of what Máirín was supposed to have said are both funny and inaccurate in equal measure. In Minnesota Máirín was supposed to have said that "the majority of people in Ireland want the means of production to be nationalised."[297] There was something most Irish people never knew. However, a lot of what the FBI wrote about Máirín was redacted in the file sent to her.

In an interview with the *San Francisco Examiner* Máirín emphasised the need for an alternative to violence. She told the paper "Improving economic conditions in the ghettos is second only to peace in our plan." Máirín spoke positively of the potential of the women led Peace Movement which was developing in the North at the time. She challenged any suggestion that she and Sinn Féin were communist claiming "anyone left of the pope

---

297 Ibid

is considered communist in Ireland." Two weeks later Máirín was speaking in New York and her topic was '*Women in Ireland*'. She returned to a familiar theme of the exploitation of women in the workforce. She said, "In all cases of discrimination against women, it is always working-class women who suffer the most because the basic discrimination is economic."[298]

Whether it was New York or Dublin, San Francisco or Belfast, Máirín kept hammering out her key messages of the need for peace and the need to combat the real problems of the capitalist economic system. It's no wonder the FBI didn't welcome Máirín as a visitor.

---

298 *San Francisco Examiner,* 11th October 1976

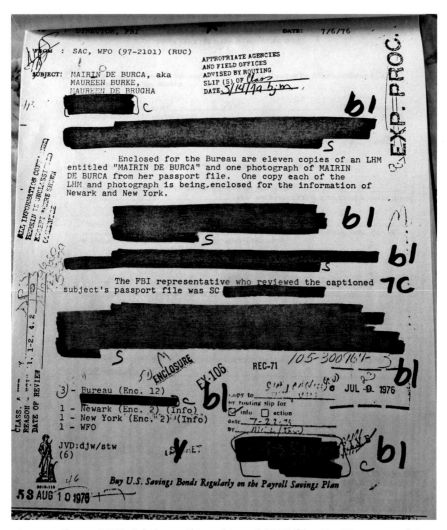

Enclosed for the Bureau are eleven copies of an LHM
entitled "MAIRIN DE BURCA" and one photograph of MAIRIN
DE BURCA from her passport file. One copy each of the
LHM and photograph is being.enclosed for the information of
Newark and New York.

The FBI representative who reviewed the captioned
subject's passport file was SC

REC-71   105-300767-   JUL 9 1976

3 - Bureau (Enc. 12)

1 - Newark (Enc. 2) (Info)
1 - New York (Enc. 2) (Info)
1 - WFO

JVD:djw/stw
(6)

Buy U.S. Savings Bonds Regularly on the Payroll Savings Plan

53 AUG 1 0 1976

12. Prisoners Rights

Whether she was in America or at an international conference, Máirín's commitment to 'her issues' back in Ireland was constant and unrelenting. Apart from her ongoing interaction with the guards and the legal system, her time in prison after the US Embassy flag burning protest certainly focused her attention on the situation of prisoners in her home country.

That six weeks ordeal had made her acutely aware of the deprivations prisoners endured and the sheer awfulness of the Irish prison system at that time. As usual, she wanted to act and became involved in the issue of prison conditions and prisoners' rights as soon as she was let out. As she simply put it,"when you saw something wrong you felt obliged to do something about it."[299]

The Politicals

Doing something, anything, for prisoners' rights in the Ireland of the 1970s was a huge undertaking. In addition to a general lack of public and political interest, governments of the day were determined not to be 'soft' on the 'politicals' - prisoners, usually from the IRA, who had been convicted of various offences, such as bank

---

299 Cathal Black film

robberies to fund their campaigns. As the 'politicals' and the 'ordinary' prisoners were sometimes mixed together, the chances of improvements in prison conditions were minimal.

Despite this, prisoners began to rebel against their primitive living conditions. Prisoners could spend most of the day locked in their cells (has anything changed?),with almost no educational or other outlets. There was no in cell toilet and prisoners had to 'slop out' every day. In the women's wing, attached to Mountjoy prison, there was only one toilet and no showers.[300] It was also reported that women prisoners weren't even allowed pencils or pens.[301]

Protests, led by the 'politicals', began to spring up in Portlaoise and Mountjoy prisons in 1972 and 1973. In one instance prison officers were held hostage as part of a campaign by prisoners for 'political status'. These protests spread to non-political prisoners and a Prisoners' Union was set up. In 1973 this organisation of prisoners led to the establishment of the Prisoners' Rights Organisation, (PRO) with Máirín De Burca as one of its leading members.

Given the political/IRA dimension to some of the protests it is not surprising that the Department of

300 Cormac Behan (2017) – *We are all convicted criminals? Prisoners, Protest and Penal Politics in the Republic of Ireland'* in Journal of Social History
301 Oisín Wall (2020) *'Embarrassing the State': The 'Ordinary' Prisoners' Rights Movement in Ireland 1972-76* in Journal of Contemporary History

Justice and the government looked on these activities with great suspicion. Paddy Cooney, a conservative Fine Gael politician, became Minister for Justice in the 1973-77 Fine Gael/Labour government. He boasted that conditions in Irish prisons compared favourably with the best in Europe.[302]

In this hostile environment one of the first challenges for the PRO was to make clear that they weren't under the control of any political organisation, a difficult task in those politically charged years. They focused on highlighting the day to day needs of prisoners and sought also to help prisoners who had been released.

Over a number of years, the PRO published their own magazine, *Jail Journal,* which detailed the daily life of prisoners. For her part Máirín didn't want the 'politicals' to have any special status. A letter she wrote to the *Irish Independent* in 1973, as the group's publicity officer, or P.R.O. for the PRO, made the position clear. It was at the time when some of the 'politicals' were engaged in a hunger strike in Mountjoy prison. She wrote "Our organisation is NOT involved in the present hunger strike … for what is called political status… We seek not the recognition of special status for an elitist group, but the immediate implementation for all prisoners of a Charter of Prisoners' Rights."[303]

---

302 Behan, op.cit.
303 *Irish Independent,* 4th October 1973

Unwelcome Visitor

Despite distancing the PRO from the 'politicals', Máirín was not a welcome visitor to Irish prisons. In 1972 she arrived at Mountjoy jail to visit a prisoner only to be told that she needed 'special permission' from the Minister (then Fianna Fail's Des O'Malley). She waited for forty five minutes and was then told permission had been refused, with no reason given.[304] It didn't come as a surprise.

The following year the Minister had changed to Fine Gael's Paddy Cooney, from the frying pan into the fire comes to mind, and Máirín was on his case. The Prisoners' Union was still in operation and Máirín asserted that prisoners were told by Cooney that "people who insisted on remaining in the union would be the last to benefit from the concessions." She went on to claim that a prisoner's membership of the Prisoners' Union would be taken into account when he/she applied for parole. These claims were denied emphatically by the Minister.[305]

What Máirín had to say and the way she said it was certainly not going to win over an already hostile Minister Cooney. However, even at that early stage, she and the PRO had decided that moderation was never going to work. Eventually the Prisoners Union faded away and the PRO became the campaigning body on behalf of prisoners.

---

304 *Irish Press,* 5th February 1972.
305 *Irish Independent,* 18th August 1973

The PRO was a consistent vocal protest and direct action organisation. They held protests, sometimes for twenty-four hours, outside different jails. They highlighted the need for rehabilitation and medical treatment and Máirín claimed that "roughly three quarters of the people in Irish prisons need proper psychiatric treatment."[306]

Jail Journal

Over a five-year period, from 1974 to 1979, *Jail Journal* detailed the many issues confronting prisoners. In its second edition it noted that "the journal is written mostly by prisoners and ex-prisoners. Some of the articles had to be smuggled out of jail at the risk of punishment. *The Journal* will have to be smuggled back in as it is banned in every prison in Ireland. So much for Civil Rights!"[307]

Jail Journal detailed the harsh and cruel conditions experienced by prisoners – the one hour a day for exercise, the eight ounces of bread and a cup of tea for breakfast, two books to read a week and punishment if you were caught swapping them. For women it was even worse, no pens, pencils or paper; no education for the many who were illiterate; no proper exercise, no games and absolutely no fun.

---

306 ibid
307 *Jail Journal*, Vol 1, No2 – Prisoners' Rights Organisation (no date)

Front cover of an edition of the Jail Journal. c.1974.

The issue of suicides in prisons was highlighted by the *Jail Journal* in 1975, noting that there had been four prison suicides in a 21-month period. *Jail Journal* claimed that the Minister for Justice called these deaths 'brainstorms' or 'mental aberrations'.[308] Even Cooney's colleagues in Fine Gael objected to his choice of words.

The PRO went further than the prison walls when they also argued that the laws and the justice system favoured the better off. Their arguments usually fell on deaf ears. In an address to the Prison Officers Association Paddy Cooney made clear "that as long as I am Minister for

308*Jail Journal*, Vol 1, No 7 – Prisoners' Rights Organisation (no date)

Justice these people will not be given recognition of any kind."[309] In return, the Prison Officers Association labelled (the PRO) as a 'mafia type organisation'[310] So, if you spoke on behalf of prisoners you were either a subversive, a member of the mafia or probably both.

Undermining

Concerted efforts were made at government level to undermine the PRO. The Minister of the day regularly tried to 'muddy the waters' and categorise all protesting prisoners as subversives. Those who did stand up were often denied recreation or even put on a bread and water diet.[311]

As well as *Jail Journal* being banned in prisons, attempts were made also to prevent PRO members visiting prisoners. Ongoing efforts were made to link the PRO with the Official IRA and Official Sinn Féin. Máirín's position as Sinn Féin general secretary made her an easy target and a statement she made in August 1974 certainly didn't help.

She referred to a jailbreak from Portlaoise prison and said that security issues in Irish jails were "not caused by prisoners but by the political situation in the country." The statement was reported to have been made on behalf

---

309 ibid
310 Wall, op. cit.
311 ibid

of the PRO and seemed to contradict the letter she had written just a year earlier. The PRO responded to Máirín's comments by emphasising that the organisation was non- political. They also made clear that their then press officer was a man called Alfred Jones and not Máirín De Burca.[312] A slap on the wrist for Máirín.

At the best of times, it is difficult to get public support for prisoners' rights and in the tense environment of the 1970s the challenges were huge. From its establishment, the PRO campaigned for some form of enquiry or investigation which would bring these issues into the public domain but got no support from the government. For his part Minister Cooney said in an RTE radio interview that there was no need for such an enquiry.[313]

Prison Reform

An Ad Hoc Committee for Prison Reform was set up in 1973, led by former prisoner Tom Bourke with other members including Joe Costello, who went on to become a TD, Conal Gibbons and Pat McCartan, law students at the time who went on to become senior judges.

Prisoner protests continued to be met with hostility and punishment. A protest in Portlaoise prison led to the leaders being transferred to the Curragh Military Detention Centre, with a bread and water diet. Beyond

---

312 *Evening Herald,* 27th August 1974
313 *Irish Press,* 6th November 1973

the prison walls Máirín and her colleagues kept up their campaign of protest. Pickets were held outside the prisons, the Department of Justice and even a dinner dance being addressed by Minister Cooney. The group went as far as picketing the home of the civil servant responsible for prisons. This protest led to a High Court injunction being granted against six of their members.[314]

While the protests were direct and 'in your face', they also continued to give ammunition to Paddy Cooney to label the participants as 'people who have subversive tendencies'.[315] The PRO challenged Cooney to produce evidence of their subversive nature, but none was forthcoming. In a statement the PRO asserted that what Cooney had said about them was "a red herring, to try to divert the attention of the public from the main issues involved in the recent suicides which occurred in prisons for which he is responsible."[316]

Portlaoise Protests

The campaign for prisoners' rights was not helped by the frequent protests and violent confrontation in Portlaoise prison where most republican prisoners were held. In 1976 four prisoners received a six-month jail sentence for injuring a warder in Portlaoise.[317] The 1973 -77 coalition government was so concerned about the situation that

---

314 *Evening Herald,* 16th May 1975
315 *Irish Press,* 19th May 1975
316 *Irish Press,* 19th May 1975
317 *Irish Independent,* 15th June 1976

they sought to bring in new rules which would allow the Minister for Justice decide who could or couldn't visit prisoners. This power included the right to stop certain legal advisors from visiting their clients. The grounds put forward were issues of security but there was a huge reaction to the proposal.

Máirín and her colleagues saw this move as a direct infringement of civil liberties and the legal profession weighed in, describing it as using a sledgehammer to crack a nut. For his part Cooney claimed that he knew of three solicitors who "have abused the privileges which normally attends legal visits." He accused these unnamed solicitors of taking letters from subversive prisoners to other subversives.[318]

Given Cooney's hostility toward the PRO it was more than surprising that during his time in office he agreed to discuss prison and Garda matters with a delegation from Sinn Féin, which included Máirín and party activist Peigín Doyle. This time Máirín entered the Dáil through the front gate but did not succeed in getting the Minister to embrace any of her suggestions. The meeting took place after the 1973 General Election and, given that Official Sinn Féin had contested the election, this was perhaps a recognition of their return to parliamentary politics.

---

318 *Irish Press,* 22nd March 1976

Pat McCartan

In 1975 solicitor Pat McCartan was Secretary of the PRO. He had asked Cooney could the PRO join groups who would be allowed visit the prisons. In his reply the Minister's private secretary wrote "The Minister has not yet decided on the composition of the groups to visit our Penal Institutions... but it is unlikely your organisation will be invited to participate."[319] This was hardly surprising as McCartan was one of the three legal advisors in the Minister's sights. He was also a member of Official Sinn Féin.

McCartan had been denied access to a prison to inspect a location relevant to a charge against one of his prisoner clients. The governor of Portlaoise prison said in an affidavit that McCartan had made a visit to his client Eddie Gallagher in October 1976 but he (the governor) was not aware that Gallagher had any outstanding legal business with the courts and went on to suggest that when McCartan visited his client the following month that he "should clarify beforehand the general nature of his business with Gallagher."[320] Gallagher was serving a twenty year sentence for his kidnapping of Dutch industrialist Teide Herrema.

It sounded and was draconian and can probably only be understood by those who lived through the politically charged period of the 1970s. However, times change

---

319 Dept. of Justice Letter to Pat McCartan, 17th October 1975, De Burca archive
320 *Irish Press*, 16th December 1976

and it is ironic to note that, over twenty years later, McCartan was appointed a Circuit Court judge. One can only imagine what some of the older mandarins in the Department of Justice must have thought.

Karl Crawley

The PRO continued, via its *Jail Journal* magazine and other means, to highlight the situation of individual prisoners. The most high profile of these was the sad case of Karl Crawley, who was regularly before the courts. Crawley was a clearly mentally ill prisoner who needed psychiatric care not a prison sentence. During his time in and out of prison he had attempted suicide on multiple occasions. District Justice Herman Good said, when Crawley appeared before him, that this case was one of the saddest he had ever come across.[321] The PRO wrote that "Help and treatment, sympathy and understanding, not punishment cells, handcuffs and sedation is what we demand for Karl Crawley and others like him."[322]

In July 1975, on one of his many court appearances, Crawley was charged with assaulting a guard (for which charge he was later acquitted). Máirín and other members of the PRO picketed outside the court and during a break went as far as placing leaflets on the jury members' seats pleading Crawley's case. The leaflet was headed 'Prison and the Mentally Ill' and stated that the medical profession and the courts had neglected their

321 *Jail Journal*, Vol 1, No. 7 – Prisoners, Rights Organisation (No date)
322 *ibid*

responsibility towards prisoners. It claimed "In the courts, psychiatric assessment is rarely used... There is no system of screening prisoners on arrival at prisons, despite the high rate of mentally ill offenders.... Even when the defendant has a long history of mental illness his record is seldom consulted and when it is it has little bearing on his sentence."[323] The leaflet was direct, informed and had Máirín's writing style all over it.

Maurice Sheehan a socially concerned twenty-year-old law student, joined the picket. He wasn't an active member of the PRO but had heard about the case and knew that Crawley should not have been in prison. While Sheehan looked up to Máirín he wouldn't have known that some of the protestors had gone into the jury box to place leaflets about the case.[324]

That action was, of course, a step too far for the legal system. The police van arrived and the guards told them all to get in. The indomitable Mrs. Gaj told the guards to get lost and that she was perfectly capable of walking around the corner to the Bridewell police station.[325]

Court Appearance

The protestors became the first people to be arrested under Section 4 of the 1972 Offences Against the State Act where the charge was in respect of "taking part in a

323 *The Irish Times*, 16th October 1975
324 Maurice Sheehan interview
325 Ibid

demonstration that constituted an interference with the court of justice."[326] After they were charged, Sheehan's parents received visits from the Garda Special Branch and on one occasion his mother kindly invited them in for tea.[327]

When the protestors came before the court Máirín read a long, prepared statement. She said "I do not believe Karl Crawley is a criminal… I believe that persons who are incapable of a specified level of rational behaviour are in need of medical care, not punishment… I make no apology for demanding that a poor, deprived and retarded young man be treated with humanity and decency." Máirín pointed out that Crawley had "done grievous harm to his person in suicide attempts and has spent many terms in Dundrum Mental Hospital under heavy sedation."[328] She then admitted that she was the one who put the leaflets in the jury box. It was no surprise that Máirín's argument fell on deaf ears.

Most of the protestors pleaded not guilty but were sentenced to twelve months imprisonment by Máirín's regular sparring partner, Justice Ó Huadhaigh.

Appeal

The sentence was appealed to the Circuit Criminal Court and Judge Roe prefaced his decision by strongly

---

326 *Irish Independent*, 19th July 1975
327 Maurice Sheehan interview
328 *The Irish Times*, 19th July 1975

criticising the protestors. He suggested that the leaflets they distributed which referred to Crawley's prison record might prejudice a jury against Crawley. He referred also to the leaflet suggesting the jury should enquire about the defendant's medical history. In Judge Roe's view "That was a terrible thing to tell a jury, to expect them to ask such questions. I never in my life read anything like this. It is completely prejudicial to the unfortunate man it was intended to help."[329]

After that broadside the PRO defendants must have feared the worst. But at the end of his 'lecture' Judge Roe said he was influenced by what barrister Mary Robinson had said on behalf of Máirín and her colleagues. He noted it was the first time a case had been brought under Section 4 of the 1972 Offences Against the State (Amendment) Act and gave all the accused the benefit of the Probation Act.[330]

On legal advice, Sheehan had his case tried separately. He pleaded guilty and was given a twelve-month suspended sentence. After the other appeals were heard, his barrister, Patrick McEntee, went back into court and Sheehan's sentence was also reduced to the Probation Act. Sheehan's mother was not put off by all of the legal actions against her son. When the whole affair died down, she attended meetings of the PRO and joined them on a protest march to Mountjoy prison.[331]

---

329 *The Irish Times,* 12th November 1975
330 ibid
331 Maurice Sheehan interview

Uphill Battle

Another important campaigning theme of the PRO was what *Jail Journal* bluntly described as 'Garda violence' against people arrested. On occasion the magazine also got anonymous contributions from prison officers, who complained about their own working conditions, a corrupt staff appointment process and victimisation if they raised their voices. Similarly, any prisoner seen to be associated with the PRO often found themselves subject to punishment.

From time to time Máirín donned the hat of 'Sinn Féin Spokeswoman for Justice' to make public comment on the treatment of people in Garda custody. She suggested that they be allowed see their own doctor, but this was dismissed by Minister Cooney who didn't accept that the Gardaí were mistreating anybody. In a letter to the *Irish Press* Máirín pointed out that "if persons in custody never have cause to complain against Garda behaviours, then the Gardaí have nothing to fear."[332] It was, of course, a logical point to make but Máirín in 1976 was up against a Minister who could only think of suppressing subversion.

Hunger Strike

In 1977 fifty prisoners went on hunger strike in Mountjoy to protest against conditions in the prison. They claimed that in the first three months of 1977, ten prisoners had

---

332 *Irish Press*, 10 September 1976

attempted suicide. For their troubles they were sentenced to two months solitary confinement.

Máirín and her ex-prisoner colleagues knew only too well how isolating and boring prison life could be, stuck in your cell, often alone, with nothing to do. In 1978 the PRO offered to give some books to the library in Mountjoy. They were rebuffed, with then Fianna Fail Minister Gerry Collins regarding it as a propaganda exercise.[333] Maybe the Minister thought they were offering copies of Mao's Little Red Book?

Collins was as strongly opposed to the PRO as his predecessor Paddy Cooney. In 1979 he made the extraordinary claim in the Dáil that the PRO "has not shown any real interest in the prisoners themselves but rather they are bringing the whole prison system to its knees."[334] In what was a considered response, the PRO claimed that Collins was the first Minister to build a prison for children, that he was building two new custodial prisons for juveniles and had plans to build a new prison for women. It was a war of words that probably got the PRO precisely nowhere. In an indication of what the PRO were up against in the 1970s they had to publicly oppose a suggestion from Justice Denis Pringle that birching replace imprisonment as punishment for juvenile offenders.[335]

---

333 *Irish Press*, 15th February 1978
334 *Irish Press*, 22nd November 1979
335 *Irish Press*, 21st February 1978

Women's Prison

In 1977 the PRO presented their demands for a public enquiry into the whole prison system, with a petition signed by over 10,000 people. It was rejected by Gerry Collins who in opposition had supported the idea of some form of enquiry. Despite nearly all their suggestions being dismissed, the PRO showed all the determination that Máirín had demonstrated during her many years of struggle in Sinn Féin. Although she left the party in the summer of 1977 Máirín continued her involvement on the issue of prisoners' rights. It was something she felt strongly about and was prepared to keep working at to effect change. In November 1977 she wrote to *The Irish Press* pointing out that various responsible journalists were agreed on one issue and have "one and all condemned the women's prison thus vindicating something I and the women who went to prison with me condemned on our release."[336]

Máirín went on to criticise the plan to build a new prison for women which would cost millions and all for about thirty prisoners. She advocated a non-custodial probation and welfare approach. Máirín lost that argument and a new women's prison on the Mountjoy jail site was developed at a cost of €13 million euro and with a capacity for eighty prisoners. It opened in 1999.

---

336 *The Irish Press*, 16th November 1977

Commission of Enquiry

In 1979 the PRO got fed up asking and set up its own Commission of Enquiry into the prison system, chaired by Seán McBride, the eminent civil rights advocate and Nobel prize winner. Among its members were two people, Mary Robinson and Michael D. Higgins, who later were to become Presidents of Ireland. The Commission held public hearings, consulted with different interests and produced its findings the following year.

Members of the PRO picket outside the Bank of Ireland in Dublin calling for a public enquiry into the prison system. Máirín is 2nd from the front.c.1976 De Burca archive.

Among its recommendations were an increase in the age of criminal responsibility to fourteen, the use of non-custodial measures for women prisoners and improvements in educational facilities for young people.

It could hardly be described as a radical agenda but getting the government to act on it was another matter. It proved to be a long and largely fruitless wait.

In 1984 the government established its own commission on prison reform, chaired by former senior civil servant T.K. Whitaker. It published its report in 1985 and it turned out to be a damning indictment of successive government policies. In essence Whitaker found that locking up prisoners was both very expensive and ineffective in deterring them from crime. The report called for an emphasis on the rehabilitation of prisoners and the use of prison as a last resort. The report called for an independent prison board to be set up, removing day to day management from the Department of Justice.

The report's recommendations could have been written by the PRO itself. It seemed, at last, that the voice of prisoners was being heard. However, recommendations are one thing and action is another. Through the 1980s and 1990s some improvements did occur, and it is to the credit of the PRO and passionate advocates such as Máirín De Burca that they kept the huge problems of our prison system in the public and political consciousness.

However, in 2010, twenty-five years after the Whitaker report, it was sobering and depressing to see a former Coordinator of Education in the prison system claim that "virtually all the core recommendations (in the Whitaker report) have been ignored.[337] There have been some further improvements since then, but, to paraphrase WB Yeats, changes in our prison system comes dropping slow.

---

337 *Irish Examiner*, 7th September 2010

13. End of the Road

At times Máirín must have wondered which parts of her job were more difficult – fighting for prison reform, campaigning for improved housing conditions, or dealing with the endless internal battles in her party.

The struggle for the 'ideological soul' of Official Sinn Féin continued on a seemingly endless journey through most of the 1970s. Leading lights such as Eoghan Harris, Eamon Smullen, Sean Garland and Eoin Ó Murchú pushed to make the party clearly dedicated to the class struggle. An 'Industrial Department' was set up within the party and gave support to the industrialisation of Ireland, and the consequent creation of a stronger working class.

Industrial Revolution

The Irish Industrial Revolution, published in 1977, was a key policy document of the party which proposed a large expansion in state employment and full employment over the course of the next decade. Tony Heffernan was one of those with reservations. "The instincts of people like myself was to oppose multinationals coming in to exploit the country".[338]

---

338 Kenny, op cit, ch 6

Relations between Máirín and the secretive grouping that controlled the party's Industrial Department were never good and in 1976 and 1977 they went from bad to worse. This grouping had a very clear view of the direction they wanted the party to go. They were particularly anxious to distance Official Sinn Féin from anything which had a 'Green' or 'Provo' tinge.

The party was involved in the Irish Council for Civil Liberties (ICCL) which was considering giving its support to a symbolic hunger strike in Portlaoise Prison. Máirín learnt that her party colleague, Eamon Smullen, was organising block voting on this issue within the ICCL, but with no mandate from the party. Máirín regarded Smullen as 'Stalinist to the nth degree... he did things that weren't democratic.'

Sinn Féin – The Workers Party

More significantly, when it came to the 1976/1977 Árd Fheis, Heffernan, Máirín and the delegates were welcomed with a large backdrop which read 'Sinn Féin-The Workers Party'. In their biography of the party, Hanley and Millar write that there was 'no dissension' within the delegates to ratifying the name change. However, Tony Heffernan was "mightily pissed off at the time. There was a motion down for debate to change the name, but when we walked in we were met with a fait accompli."[339]

---

339 ibid

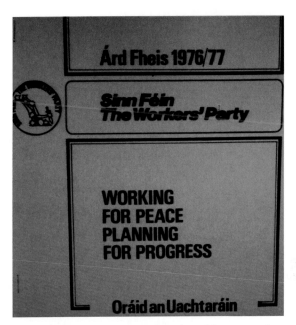

*Front cover of the party President's address to the 1976/77
Ard Fheis of the newly named party.
Tony Heffernan archive, UCD archives.*

For her part, Máirín had been concerned with the
various secret groups, or cadres, springing up in the
party. "They examined people's every word, every gesture
almost, were they Stalinist or weren't they; if they weren't
they did their damnedest to get them out of the party."[340]
Although they were joint general secretaries, neither
Heffernan nor Máirín felt they were being fully informed
about what was going on in the party and what its full
membership was.

Almost blithely the party leadership spoke as if the
revolution was just around the corner. In his address

---

340 Hanley and Miller, ch.10

to that 1976/77 Árd Fheis, Party President Tomás MacGiolla continued to claim that Sinn Féin "is the party of the workers and we have the policies which can build a Democratic Socialist Republic."[341] Predictable Árd Fheis stuff, designed to rally the troops, but at this stage Máirín was beginning to look at the door marked Exit. Notwithstanding this, she kept working away, dealing with all the familiar issues that crossed her desk - housing, evictions, prisoners' rights.

Máirín attends a meeting in Finglas with Proinsias De Rossa on housing. It was one of her last public events before her resignation. It is highly unlikely that De Rossa added the 'take a letter' inscription. 1977.

---

341 *Presidents Address, Sinn Féin Árd Fheis,* 1976/77, Tony Heffernan archive, UCD archives

General Election

Before Máirín finalised her decision to leave the party, there was the matter of a general election which took place in June 1977. Máirín was well established in the Dublin North Central constituency and respected for her 'on the ground' work on housing and other local issues. She was the obvious candidate. However, the party's Industrial Department had other ideas. In Tony Heffernan's view, "Smullen regarded Máirín as a bit of a dilettante, involved in issues such as housing and women, whereas the core issue was industrialise, industrialise and the creation of a strong working class".[342]

Des Geraghty totally disagreed with the efforts to get someone to run instead of Máirín, "we should have been backing her to the hilt." Geraghty was subsequently told by an Irish journalist who worked in Russia "that my name was in Moscow, and I was described as a social democrat who was a danger to the party."[343]

Despite Máirín being the obvious and best candidate, party infighting led to her being replaced by a man called Ray McGrann and he performed very poorly. Máirín's colleague and then *Irish People* editor Padraig Yeates believed Máirín could have become a TD. "I canvassed very hard for her … She would have won a Dáil and Council seat I've no doubt. She had tremendous loyalty in some communities."[344]

---

342 Tony Heffernan Interview
343 Des Geraghty interview
344 Padraig Yeates interview

Yeates recalls a no holds barred campaign in Máirín's constituency and on one occasion anonymous posters appeared with the slogan 'O'Brien's Black Bastards', referring to Labour candidate Conor Cruise O'Brien who had adopted children from Africa. While regarding Máirín as a very tough woman on issues she believed in, Yeates believed she wasn't equally tough in advancing her own career, "She wasn't that type of person."[345]

While colleagues were unhappy at Máirín not being the party candidate, the woman herself was more sanguine and had recognised that electoral politics was not for her. In any event she had more important issues on her mind, such as giving up her job as party general secretary. A number of factors came together. 'There was the makings of another split… we had these Industrial Department people coming in and dictating to everybody… I had done everything I wanted to do and maybe it was time to haul myself off. I thought I'm not heading into another split.'

Departure

Many people thought Máirín's decision to leave the party was because she wasn't selected as the election candidate, but she is very clear that wasn't the case. 'That wasn't it at all as I wouldn't have been a happy candidate. I think I had burnout. I had been active for eleven years and I just needed to get out, I never regretted it.'

---

345 ibid

Tomás Mac Giolla suggested she take a long holiday but Máirín's mind was made up. 'I was just tired… It was all consuming… I was a bit sad leaving, but I knew it was the right thing to do.'

Máirín de Burca quits Sinn Féin

Former general secretary Mairin de Burca has resigned from membership of Sinn Fein — the Workers Party.

Ms de Burca told the party's Ard Comhairle that personal reasons prevented her from being an active worker and she did not wish to be just a "paper" member. Her resignation was

Newspaper headline announcing Máirín's resignation.1977

True to form Máirín didn't tell her colleagues when she was actually finishing. One Friday evening, when everyone else had gone home, she packed her belongings and left a note saying she wouldn't be back. The party issued a statement which thanked Máirín for her commitment to the party over a twenty-two-year period and noted her resignation was for 'personal reasons.' They were probably at least half right. Whatever the reasons or motivation, at the age of just thirty-nine Máirín De Burca's formal political career was suddenly over.

Assessment

Máirín was active in Sinn Féin from 1954 to 1977. It was a period which incorporated the 'Border Campaign', the move back to electoral politics, the split with Provisional Sinn Féin, the conflict in the North and the leftward move of the party, which became Sinn Féin: The Workers Party just before she resigned her position as General Secretary.

For most of those twenty-three years Máirín worked hard to change Sinn Féin into a party which was focused on issues of social justice and equality and not just the national question. She helped move the party to 'the left' and into campaigns on a variety of important issues.

With regard to the national question, apart from her youthful flirtation, Máirín was a constant and brave critic of the use of physical force. She spoke against it on many occasions and at times put herself at risk. By any measure, therefore, her contribution to left wing and democratic politics has to be seen as significant.

In a newspaper interview after she retired Máirín had just come from an 'overnight stay' in Mountjoy for non-payment of a fine. Nothing new there. She expressed some disappointment that she couldn't stay longer. "It was a pity really. I wanted to stay in for a few days to see what conditions in the 'Joy were like. But I had a few things to do, and I had to make sure the cat was fed." With more than a hint of irony she said that "the nightdresses are getting decidedly sexy."[346]

Máirín continued to be relaxed and at ease about her decision to leave Sinn Féin "You could say I am like a girl who got married at 16, lived happily for 23 years and has now got a judicial separation."[347] Looking back on her career in politics she once again rejected the physical violence approach. "Since 1969 I have moved further and further toward the belief that pacification is the essential step toward solving the Irish situation... Since 1969 there are 2,000 dead and we are politically worse off than ever."[348]

Máirín told the *Sunday Independent* that she planned to write a number of political articles and she had recently finished one with the title *How to prevent yourself falling down the stairs in a police station.*[349] It was the end of an extraordinarily active political career. But Máirín wasn't even forty years old and an interesting 'Second Act' was about to begin.

---

346 *Sunday Independent*, 31st July 1977
347 ibid
348 ibid
349 ibid

Family Changes

Along with Máirín's career changing there were also significant changes in the De Burca family. Her mother had become crippled with arthritis and, having completely ignored Máirín's advice, ended up having the lower part of one leg amputated and she spent the last years of her life sitting in a chair.

Her father had adjusted to retirement and spent his time around the house and socialising in Newbridge. 'Daddy would go into town and have a pint and a shot of whiskey. He was an extrovert and always wanted to be the life and soul of the party... People liked him but I don't know if he made many friends when he got home.'

Máirín's brother Michael lived almost his whole life in the family home. He never worked and once turned down a job which a social worker had found for him. 'He was smothered by his mother who never encouraged him to work. Once when he was in his 40s I asked him would he go to the cinema with me and my cousins. He said yes and then turned to Mammy and asked, 'Will I need a coat?' At which I freaked.'

Máirín's parents both died during the 1970s, with her father preceding his wife by about four years. When Máirín's mother died she left everything to her son Michael and Máirín wasn't mentioned in the will. Michael eventually moved into a nursing home in Athy where he got on well and was well looked after. He died in 2013.

14. Looking For Work

When Máirín left Sinn Féin she got what she called 'a bronze handshake' which went quickly on debt and mortgage payments. She was now unemployed and needed to find work. She moved abruptly from days of constant busyness and pressure to a totally different world.

Shortly after leaving Sinn Féin, Máirín detailed in *The Irish Times* a week in her life of job hunting and surviving on a welfare income of £9.80 a week. Like a lot of her journalism, it was funny, direct and packed a punch. For one job interview she "got into a skirt in deference to male susceptibilities…was told I could await a letter and was so depressed that I bought a bunch of flowers on the way home. They cost 90p."[350]

On the Thursday of the week Máirín went on a £7 pound 'shopping spree', with £1.50 of it spent on essential cat food. She had decided a long time ago "that if life was going to be bearable at all I would have to possess, adopt or have access to a cat or cats."[351] For another interview on the Friday the rebel reasserted herself. "Didn't bother with a skirt this time. Male susceptibilities can go hang.

---

350 *The Irish Times*, 1st September 1977
351 ibid

Interviewed by two 19-year-olds. Did I think my name would hinder the work of the organisation? You'd think I was Attila the Hun or something."[352]

Making life bearable. Máirín and her cat Whiskey. Her other cat Soda is out of sight, c.1983 De Burca archive.

A friend who had offered her a job backed out, claiming that "his partner had blankly refused to have me in the office." By the end of her week's diary Máirín gave

352 ibid

"a fleeting thought to answering an ad for job of PR with Fine Gael. At least I would have fun giving my curriculum vitae – 'I was arrested 25 times – reference Mr. Patrick Cooney' – decided against, can't afford such frivolities."[353] Getting work proved to be a hard slog but Máirín's good humour and resilience stood to her.

House Buying

As if unemployment wasn't challenging enough, with the help of Mrs. Gaj, Máirín was also buying a small cottage in Dublin's city centre. Mrs. Gaj had told Máirín previously that she would help her either to study law or to pay a deposit and stamp duty on a house. Máirín wasn't sure about the study and opted for a new home. She had been renting a flat in Dublin 4 for a long time with no lease and very little rent. When a request came to sign a lease, she knew a rent increase was on the way. It was time to move on.

In the 1970s buying a house was relatively quick and easy. Máirín headed over to Mrs Gaj one evening, with a copy of the *Evening Herald* in her pocket. The house advertisements had two cottages for sale, one was in a quiet cul-de-sac close to the city centre. The owner agreed a price of £4,500, Mrs Gaj paid the deposit and that was that. So, without too much fuss Máirín was a house owner, but she had a mortgage to repay and earning money was a priority.

---

353 Ibid

Both during and after her political career Mrs. Gaj was a constant, supportive presence in Máirín's life and indeed in the lives of many other activists. Gaj's restaurant was somewhere Máirín felt comfortable. It didn't serve alcohol which was a big plus for her as Máirín disliked "pubs, drinkers and most extroverts, with a passion composed of nine parts envy, one-part genuine revulsion."[354]

When Mrs Gaj died Máirín recalled her restaurant's role in the IWLM, seeing it as "as an integral part of our attempted social revolution... a whole generation of political activists have reason to be grateful to Margaret Gaj...it was no wonder that many of the younger ones took to calling her 'mother.'"[355]

With the help of 'Mother Gaj', Máirín spent five happy years living in her cottage and was at times able to walk home for her lunch. It was a quiet area, with only the occasional interruption. One evening an 'entrepreneurial' neighbour was seen carrying a number of boxes of televisions into his house. The enterprise was short lived when the Gardai came calling a few nights later. In contrast another neighbour played at full blast a record of the Pope's visit to Ireland in 1979. It was on twenty-four hours a day and only ended when this obsessed man died in tragic circumstances. Apart from these occasional interruptions it was a quiet neighbourhood.

354 *The Irish Times*, 3rd April 1980
355 *The Irish Times*, 7th July 2011

Employment Agencies

Máirín registered with some employment agencies but her name and reputation went before her. She had learned to type in school, but she also had a CV littered with arrests, jail sentences and protests. The biographer of the IWLM wrote that "De Burca was almost as unemployable in Ireland at the time as any suspected communist whose name was on the blacklist in 1950s America."[356]

Every morning Máirín would cross the road to the phone box in the local pub with her fistful of coins, to check if any jobs had surfaced. Few people had their own phones in those days. It was a long, unproductive slog and Máirín ended up being unemployed for the next year. Eventually, a Liverpool – Irish woman in one agency came to the rescue. She put forward Máirín for a couple of jobs, but she was rejected. She asked Máirín was there anything she should know about her and when Máirín explained her past this woman took on to fight what she saw as discrimination. Eventually a job came up with the Post Office Engineering Union. The agency sent in only two names, Máirín's and a woman who could neither type nor spell. It would be an obvious case of discrimination if Máirín wasn't selected, but she was and she moved from being a general secretary to a secretary/typist.[357]

---

356 Stopper, ch.16
357 ibid

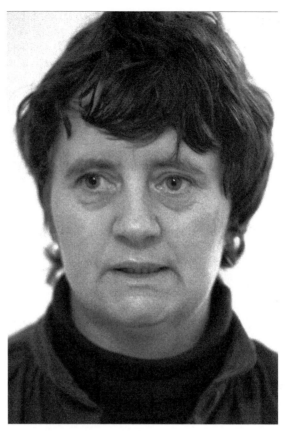

40-year-old Máirín embarks on her search for a job and a new career.1978. Photo: Derek Speirs.

Máirín took the job 'because I desperately needed work and because the agent had put so much work into finding someone to take me on, but it wasn't really what I wanted to do.' However, Máirín was now working in a union environment which suited her. Crucially, the job brought in an income. Máirín was able to pay her mortgage and had time to think about what she wanted to work at in the longer term.

Right to Bail

While Máirín may have left Sinn Féin that did not mean she had left behind the issues she felt strongly about. Her concerns about women's rights, homelessness, prisoners and the criminal justice system were constant. Máirín De Burca never really retired.

One of her ongoing battles was against any attempt to further restrict the right to bail. In August 1979 Lord Mountbatten, a relative of the British Royal Family, was brutally murdered in Sligo by the IRA. Two teenage boys and an elderly woman were also killed in the attack. There was widespread disgust across the country and calls to tighten the right to bail were made.

This issue was an uphill struggle for Máirín and less than a month after Mountbatten's murder she made her case in one of the many letters she wrote to *The Irish Times*. Her essential arguments were that there already existed restrictions on the right to bail and that the fundamental principle of the presumption of innocence must be upheld. She argued that "restrictions on bail will do nothing to improve the detection rate and this is the real problem to which the Garda Síochána and the Department of Justice should address themselves. We should not barter the civil rights of our citizens for a kind of preventive detention or internment without trial. That would indeed be a victory for the Provos."[358] Later that year she spoke at a seminar on the issue organised

---

358 *The Irish Times*, 17th September 1979

by the Irish Council for Civil Liberties. It was a debate that surfaced periodically over the next two decades. However, in 1996 a referendum on the issue was passed which led to a tightening of access to bail.

Sensitive Issue

Máirín also had the occasional opportunity to speak publicly on women's issues, an opportunity she was happy to take. At the end of 1979 she spoke on the topic 'My Kind of Feminism' at a seminar organised by the Women's Political Association (WPA). In her usual clear and direct manner she said that "the time had come for the women's movement to accept two facts of life: that women differed greatly among themselves in their opinions, and that the movement had made mistakes and would continue to make them. They could learn from these mistakes."[359]

Máirín instanced the always sensitive issue of rape and spoke about a recent march where she felt the speeches from the platform "had alienated many supporters by appearing to attack men."[360] What was said from this platform was not explained. But Máirín, despite her often confrontational approach, also emphasised the importance of bringing people with you on what were often difficult journeys.

---

359 *The Irish Times*, 4th December 1978
360 ibid

She might be one of your old friends and campaigning colleagues, but that was all put aside if Máirín disagreed with you. In 1980 Nell McCafferty called on all feminists to support the protest undertaken by women prisoners in Armagh Prison. This protest was similar to the one started by male Republican prisoners and focused on prison conditions and the criminalisation of 'political prisoners'.

For Nell it was a feminist issue, for Máirín it was not. In a newspaper article Máirín made her position clear. "I am a feminist and because I am a feminist, I refuse to support the demands of one group of women prisoners for treatment that is superior to that given to another group of political prisoners."[361] Máirín's criticism was strongly worded and ended with a direct appeal. "Yes Nell, a feminist can ask that the women in Armagh call off their dirty protest. A feminist has a right to ask that they should use the time …to give thought to the real meaning of feminism, that they would open their arms in sisterhood to the prostitutes and thieves, the child batterers and husband killers and that together they would fight for the human dignity of all prisoners. Feminism should provide no shelter for elitism."[362] Those few sentences capture well Máirín's opposition to certain forms of republicanism, to elitism and to the way society ignored the 'prostitutes and the thieves'.

---

361 *The Irish Times,* 5th September 1980
362 ibid

Apart from the issue of the Armagh women, Máirín continued her involvement with the Prisoners' Rights Organisation and in 1978 she got her knuckles gently rapped again. She had written one of her many letters to *The Irish Times* on prison conditions which brought a reply from leading member and Public Relations Officer, Joe Costello, who pointed out that "Máirín De Burca is a respected member of the PRO. However, she is not a spokesperson and the views expressed in her letter were not expressed on behalf of that organisation."[363] A respected member who found it hard to keep quiet, perhaps?

363 *The Irish Times*, 6th September 1978

15. Journalism: Hibernia

From a young age Máirín had two career ambitions. One was to be General Secretary of Sinn Féin, and the other was to be a journalist. She had done the first and now was ready for the second.

During her time working for Sinn Féin she had penned the occasional article or book review. In September 1979 she wrote a long article for *The Irish Times* in which she described with great humour her momentous decision to move from Dublin 4 to Dublin's northside. There she found "a new hate object and a hatred more sincere and more passionate than any I ever felt for the most brutal of rack renting landlords."[364] Máirín was referring to the motor car and the fact that her neighbourhood was being taken over by garages and parked cars. Her writing style was engaging and it was no surprise when a journalism opportunity emerged.

John Mulcahy

Máirín had already contributed articles and book reviews to *Hibernia* magazine, which was edited by John Mulcahy. He knew Máirín could write, and they were on the same wavelength in terms of their political and social

---

364 *The Irish Times,* 28th September 1979

outlook. When a journalist left the magazine Mulcahy talked to Máirín about joining the staff. She was keen but had one proviso and told Mulcahy that 'I will never write a sentence which in any way encourages anyone to use physical violence to achieve political ends. I knew his thinking.'

With that out of the way Máirín became a journalist with what was a punchy, left of centre magazine. It was at the beginning of the 1980s, a harsh decade with many pressing social and political issues to write about. *Hibernia* was popular but financially it was always on a knife edge. Experienced journalists such as Brian Trench and Andy Pollak worked in *Hibernia* and they and others were always pushing the boundaries.

Máirín discovered that all editors have hang ups and hobby horses. In Mulcahy's case it was Gay Byrne and Dublin Lord Mayor Carmencita Hederman. 'You couldn't praise Gaybo and you couldn't criticise Carmencita. I wrote one sentence comparing Gay favourably with someone else. Sentence deleted. I watched Carmencita chair a Dublin Corporation meeting one night and it was mayhem. She had no idea how to chair a meeting. I criticised her in my article. Sentence taken out. Anyone who says editors don't interfere…' However, there were also occasions when Máirín would simply say to her editor, 'I'm not doing that', when asked to do a particular story.

Máirín at her desk in Hibernia in 1980. Photo: Derek Speirs.

Social Affairs

Máirín worked for *Hibernia* from early 1979 until the magazine's closure in mid-1980. The issues she wrote about – housing, women, the guards and the prisons - happened to be the same ones she had campaigned on during her Sinn Féin years. Whether by accident or design, Máirín became *Hibernia's* social affairs correspondent. And while balanced in her reporting, she also had an opportunity to run a critical eye over various powerful interests.

The housing problem in Dublin featured regularly in Máirín's articles. Early on in her new job she reported that "Another chunk of land owned by a religious order has come on the property market and been sold for over £1 million." And then went on to write that "religious denominations, particularly the Roman Catholics, have used their land to make vast profits at the expense of the citizens of Dublin."[365] It was a mixture of reportage and commentary which *Hibernia* was happy to allow.

Corpo Tells Families: Breed And Be Housed

It has long been an accepted fact that couples applying to the Allocations Department of Dublin Corporation who have only one or two children are shooed away from the hatches and told to come back when they have four or five. But the ante has been upped for those families living in Corporation maisonettes; they are told that with only four children they do not have enough points for rehousing. Caught in a limbo-land of neither private nor proper Corporation housing, such families are faced with the option of breeding huge families or remaining in what were originally designed as small, temporary units. With their dilemma increased by the worsening housing crisis some of these families have now formed an action group, as MAIRIN DE BURCA reports.

The family of Michael Eastw for example, already numbers f with a fifth expected, and have been informed that this not constitute overcrowding two-bedroomed maisonette. poration officials are not too f coming on how many chil exactly the families will hav have before they qualify; don't like the situation descr as crudely as that, preferring say that the families will be bo when they acquire the requ number of points!

Already the Eastwood hom

Máirín highlights an 'innovative' approach to housing allocations in Dublin Corporation. 1979.

---

365 *Hibernia*, 22nd February 1979

In May 1979 Máirín highlighted the work of the charity Alone, which helped older people living on their own. The charity estimated there were "at least 200 old people living alone in conditions of some distress in Dublin city."[366] In October 1979 she was writing about homeless families squatting in Dublin Corporation's housing office and in the Lord Mayor's Mansion House.[367] By the end of the year, in a throwback to her earlier years, Máirín reported on the formation of a new Dublin Housing Action Committee which sought the declaration of a housing emergency and had its own six point programme. It must have all sounded very familiar.

What was somewhat different is that the City Council's own housing committee called for an emergency to be declared. Máirín rightly questioned whether this was going to make any practical difference. She noted that it was certain that "the local authority will not take over derelict or abandoned property for the use of the homeless or, even more mundanely, carry out repairs on private houses and recoup the cost from the landlords."[368]

Squatters Amnesty

The city council had a strange way of reacting to the idea of a housing emergency, because Máirín was soon reporting that there was to be no amnesty for squatters

366 *Hibernia*, 3rd May 1979
367 *Hibernia*, 25th October 1979
368 *Hibernia*, 13th December 1979

and that 501 families " must be evicted or persuaded to leave their accommodation."[369] In fairness to Máirín, she did point out that in previous years many squatters either left voluntarily or were transferred to other properties. Her central argument, however, remained unchanged, which was "the Corporation will have to provide more accommodation as the only long-term solution to the problem."[370]

For some families who actually had Corporation flats, living conditions were often dire. In an article entitled 'Bleeding to Death in Sheriff Street', Máirín described the situation in this north inner-city street which had eight blocks of Corporation flats. She listed the complete absence of basic community facilities - no post office, phone box or pharmacy - and claimed that "Parts of the area today and for many years past resemble nothing so much as Dresden in 1945."[371] It wasn't like Máirín to be so dramatic in her journalism, but she obviously felt it was warranted on this occasion. In the following years Sheriff Street and its neighbourhood eventually benefited from 'The Gregory Deal', involving local TD Tony Gregory and Taoiseach Charlie Haughey, and from other regeneration initiatives.

---

369 *Hibernia,* 31st January 1980
370 Ibid.
371 *Hibernia,* 22nd May 1980

A woman's best friend. Máirín at home in her cottage with Spooky. c. 1977. De Burca archive.

As part of her ongoing analysis of Dublin's housing crisis, Máirín wrote about the fallout from Fianna Fail's populist but disastrous decision to abolish domestic rates in 1977 without coming up with any alternative source of income for local authorities. She wrote "There were many who claimed that the abolition of rates was madness and that a legitimate source of income should never be cut off by any provident government."[372] No doubt Máirín was among the 'many', but as a reporter there was only so far she could go. In any event, she was now enjoying a relatively quiet life, with regular working hours and more time for herself.

Artisan Dwellings

During her campaigning days private landlords were often in Máirín's sights. In *Hibernia* she put the spotlight on the company which in 1979 was to become the capital's biggest private landlord. Folio Homes was acquiring 651 artisan homes, all of them rent controlled. Dublin Artisan Dwellings, a charity, was moving out of the sector and this private company had stepped in to take its place.[373]

There were understandable concerns among tenants, even if they were paying controlled rents. That concern was exacerbated a year later when Máirín reported on a key judgement in the High Court which found sections of the Rent Restrictions Act to be unconstitutional. The court challenge was taken by Patrick Madigan, a well-known landlord, and it resulted in years of political debate while the legislators tried to deal with the court's decision.

---

372 *Hibernia*, 6th March 1980
373 *Hibernia*, 14th June 1979

Máirín was an effective chronicler of her times and the harsh conditions some people in Dublin had to endure. She described in detail some of the appalling conditions Travellers (known also as itinerants in those years) had to endure. In 1978 over 1,000 families were still living on the road, with many "official sites resembling nothing as much as American – Indian reservations." In a message which was all too familiar, Máirín wrote that "The failure of local communities to welcome Travelling families into their midst and the resultant reluctance of Travellers to want to settle on terms of derision and discrimination has produced a kind of stalemate in the problem."[374] Given the ongoing hostility which met many proposed halting sites for Travellers, describing it as 'a kind of stalemate' was a considerable understatement. Máirín's journalism benefited from this approach - lower key, factual and with well-aimed barbs included.

Reporting Women

Whenever she could Máirín wrote about women - their issues, their concerns and their struggles. And there was plenty of them to go round. The related issues of equal pay and equal employment opportunities, which she had campaigned on both in the IWLM and in the trade union movement, were far from being resolved despite the passing of equal pay legislation some years earlier. Máirín often wrote about cases being brought before Equality Officers on the issue.

---

374 *Hibernia*, 10th April 1980

In one article she described a dispute at Dublin Airport involving women cleaners as being the 'unlikely battlefield' for "the last battle of male chauvinism against equal employment opportunities for women."[375] Máirín was not simplistic in her analysis as she noted also that an important part of the dispute was being fought "in the teeth of bitter opposition from the Irish Transport and General Workers Union (ITGWU)"[376] which represented male workers in the dispute. As Máirín acknowledged it was a complicated matter but she ended her article by pointing out, "in the meantime, the women picket the airport in a battle for jobs that was supposed to have been won several years ago."[377]

Women in Politics

While not writing about politics as such, Máirín was sometimes given the job of writing about women in politics. It was somewhat sexist, but she ran with it. In the aftermath of the 1979 local and European elections she looked carefully at the results to see if such a thing as a 'women's vote' existed at all. Her forensic examination of the results led her to conclude that "if there was any woman's vote this time out it was miniscule and that it seldom crossed party boundaries and further that it made no demand on feminist issues." In the European elections she described the vote for Fianna Fail candidate

375 *Hibernia*, 21st June 1979
376 Ibid.
377 ibid

Síle De Valera as little more than "apostolic succession with little to do with politics or feminism."

Sometimes the feminist in Máirín had to be let out and she finished her analysis by writing that "in the recent elections there is some but by no means overwhelming evidence of a woman's vote. There was no evidence at all of a feminist vote and that is why the party leaders remain happy and assured."[378] So, if they got around to reading Máirín's article, Taoiseach Jack Lynch and soon to be Taoiseach Charlie Haughey could sleep easy in their beds.

Máirín examines the concept of a 'women's vote after the 1979 local and European elections.

378 *Hibernia*, 21st June 1979

Although there wasn't to be a general election until 1981, the process of candidate selection was underway in 1979. Máirín examined the well-established pattern of family members 'inheriting' a parent's Dáil seat. It usually passed from father to son but now daughters were getting in on the act. In Cork Myra Barry sought to replace her father, Dick Barry. In Clare Madeline Taylor had already taken her father's County Council seat and awaited his retirement from the Dáil. In Dublin, Mary Cosgrave was "making a name for herself despite her father's (Liam Cosgrave, former Taoiseach) old fashioned notions about women and their place."[379]

Máirín was sympathetic to this development. She wrote that "things are changing. Not only are women demanding such basic rights as equal pay, but also the right to be considered as serious contenders for public office. The fact that many such women are daughters of sitting politicians should not be used to denigrate the leap forward that their emergence signifies."[380]

Máirín was also realistic enough to know that women politicians didn't necessarily lead to change in the rights of women. She was quick to point out that "None of the three major parties took a stand for immediate equal pay, none of them is prepared to give women an unequivocal right to plan their own families, to get divorced, or to fair taxation when married."[381] Nearly twenty years on from

---

379 *Hibernia*, 16th August 1979
380 ibid
381 ibid

the IWLM what Máirín wrote was depressingly accurate.

Despite her sympathetic approach to female candidates, Máirín wasn't going to give any of them a free pass. Before the general election came round, Dick Barry's twenty-two-year-old daughter Myra Barry won a by election and became the country's youngest TD.

In an interview, Máirín got the young Myra Barry to admit that she would prefer people not to use contraception and that she favoured the 'natural method'. It was clear to Máirín that Myra Barry "feels no burning injustice on behalf of her sex."[382] Máirín clearly was not impressed. However, Myra Barry topped the poll in four successive elections until she retired from politics before she was thirty.

Poverty and Politics

Apart from the 'women in politics' issue, Máirín steered, or was steered, clear of political reporting. Given her background it made sense. There were times, however, when politics and social issues overlapped. In the early 1970s, on the initiative of Minister of State and Labour TD Frank Cluskey, a Combat Poverty scheme had been set up to initiate various pilot programmes to tackle the problem. Its chairperson was Sr. Stanislaus (later she became known as Sr. Stan) Kennedy, who was Ireland's best known anti-poverty campaigner. Cluskey was a

382 *Hibernia*, 22nd November 1979

Minister of State in the 1973-77 Coalition government but when Fianna Fail came to power in 1977, things began to change.

In a number of articles Máirín detailed the work of Combat Poverty and explained that Sr. Stanislaus did not want to get "involved in simple charity; poverty means exclusion and a sense of powerlessness and worthlessness. She (Sr. Stanislaus) sees the major work of Combat Poverty Projects as being to give the poor a sense of their own worth and power."[383]

Máirín was probably in agreement with those sentiments, but the new Taoiseach, Charlie Haughey, certainly wasn't. By early 1980 Máirín reported that the Combat Poverty budget had been cut and that this "is almost certainly the beginning of the end for Combat Poverty."[384]

Haughey was Minister for Social Welfare before becoming Taoiseach and would have been responsible for funding the organisation. He had already insisted that any references in Combat Poverty literature to 'redistribution of resources', or 'changes in the social, economic and political systems', were to be removed.[385] There was to be none of that radical nonsense when Haughey was in charge. Having previously called Fr. Michael Sweetman 'a gullible priest' one can only imagine what words he used to describe Sr. Stanislaus.

---

383 *Hibernia,* 22nd November 1979
384 *Hibernia,* 28th February 1980
385 *Hibernia,* 3rd April 1980

Máirín's articles helped keep the difficulties Combat Poverty experienced, and their efforts to have funding restored, in the public mind. Rather optimistically she wrote that "We may yet see members of St. Vincent De Paul, Trócaire and the Committee of Combat Poverty on the barricades."[386] Combat Poverty survived and the volatile political situation at the time probably helped. Haughey's first term as Taoiseach lasted less than two years and his government was dissolved in June 1981. It's hard to imagine Máirín shedding too many tears.

Justice Issues

Given the type of magazine *Hibernia* was, and Máirín's interests, it was inevitable that articles about the guards and the prisons appeared under her by line. Her old adversary Gerry Collins was still Minister for Justice. One of Máirín's first articles for *Hibernia* was about Collins' refusal to adequately fund the Free Legal Advice Centres (FLAC) and develop a proper system of legal aid across the country. Cute politician that he was Collins kept his head down on the issue while David Andrews, his Minister of State, bluntly told FLAC that if their centres closed "It will be on your consciences."

Máirín pointed to government Green and White papers which suggested budget cuts in social services and concluded that "FLAC and its work are merely the first

---

386 Ibid

victim of this anti - poor mentality."[387] Despite these depressing messages FLAC survived but it wasn't until the mid 1990s that a state-run legal aid scheme was introduced.

In the few years since Máirín left Sinn Féin, prison conditions had remained unchanged and discontent among prisoners and staff often came to the boil. A riot took place in 1978 in St. Patrick's Institution for young offenders and a small number of prison officers were transferred as a result of their behaviour.

Máirín writes about a familiar subject, prison conditions in Mountjoy. 1979.

---

387 *Hibernia*, 8th February 1979

In February 1980 Máirín was able to report on another riot in the same institution and, via her sources in the PRO, she suggested this may have been provoked by prison officers for their own, unspecified ends. Gerry Collins remained silent but claimed he had a press statement ready, but no one asked him for it. What he certainly didn't do was allow himself to be questioned by Máirín.

From time-to-time Máirín highlighted individual cases as a way of exposing the fault lines in the whole justice system. One was a former prisoner called Dessie Keane who ended up working in the Department of Agriculture. After talking about his experience of prison on an RTE programme, Keane received a letter from the Department telling him that his temporary contract was being terminated. Other temporary staff were not treated in the same way so it was clear Keane was being targeted.

Máirín could do little except highlight this young man's experience. She saw Keane's dismissal "as an act of petty revenge which is denying a young man a chance to rehabilitate himself… His sacking is no doubt also meant as a warning to others to keep their mouths shut about prison conditions unless they wish to suffer a similar fate."[388]

Then there was the case of fifteen-year-old Aidan White. This young boy had been arrested and held in Dundrum

---

388 *Hibernia*, 15th February 1979

Garda station in south Dublin for nearly 48 hours without his mother being told. His right to have a parent present when questioned was ignored. Aidan White became ill in custody and later died. Máirín reported that "During his 48 hours in police custody he had only one meal of any substance and, apart from that, snacks of tea and biscuits."[389] Significantly, Máirín went on to point out that the "State pathologist admitted that hunger could have aggravated the meningitis from which the boy died."[390]

Given this tragic outcome, Justice Minister Collins was forced to make a statement in the Dáil where he said that thirteen Gardaí 'Failed to act as they should have done.' Collins said he had 'conveyed this concern… to the Garda authorities'. But as Máirín pointed out, "Whatever steps, if any, are taken by the Garda authorities, they will not be revealed to the public. The Aidan White case is now closed."[391]

In a similar vein Máirín wrote about Michael Joseph Kavanagh who had gone to the High Court claiming he had been 'beaten, kicked, half suffocated with a plastic bag and deliberately burned with matches by Gardaí' while being held in Crumlin Garda station. Kavanagh was on bail awaiting trial on a robbery charge when the alleged assault took place. Máirín presented Kavanagh's accusations in great detail but these were denied by

389 *Hibernia*, 22nd January 1979
390 ibid
391 *Hibernia*, 22nd November 1979

Gardai in court. It seemed to be a case of 'He said/She said', but in any event the judge decided, on a technical issue, that he didn't need to rule on whether the assaults took place or not.[392] Absolutely no comfort for Michael Kavanagh and undoubtedly frustrating for Máirín.

Despite all Máirín's campaigning for the rights of prisoners and people in custody her articles in *Hibernia* revealed a continuation of systems and institutions where there were some appalling practices and zero accountability.

Closure

Hibernia always pushed the boundaries of what it could write about and as a result ended up dealing with a number of libel cases. In the end it ran out of road, and money, and was forced to close its doors in 1980. Máirín enjoyed her spell with *Hibernia* and her new career. 'I was quite good, good at meeting deadlines and I enjoyed meeting people. It was quite a tragedy when it went as you need that type of independent journalism. But you need money. John Mulcahy was upset when he came in to tell us it was closing. We were all made redundant.'

Máirín was a member of the National Union of Journalists (NUJ) which tried hard to get a decent redundancy payment for the staff. Her old colleague Padraig Yeates was secretary of Máirín's branch and

---

392 *Hibernia*, 13th March 1980

knew Mulcahy to be "tight fisted. It was like getting blood out of a stone." (Yeates went on to be a journalist with *The Irish Times* and the author of a number of books on labour and social history. Apart from that, his 'claim to fame' was that Charlie Haughey had liked his book on the 1913 Lock Out and asked Yeates to write an account of the formation of his first government. They met in Haughey's palatial home in north county Dublin and discussed Yeates' fee among other things. In the end the book didn't happen, but Yeates consoled himself afterwards by thinking "I must be the only person in Ireland who goes to Charlie Haughey *and he offers me money*.")[393]

Máirín could rightfully look back on her first foray into journalism with some satisfaction. In her two years with *Hibernia,* she had written about housing, poverty, women's inequality, Garda abuse and prison riots. Those years were grim ones in Ireland and in Dublin. If any future historian wants to know about social conditions in the country in 1979 and 1980 they would certainly benefit from reading Máirín De Burca's journalism.

And while she may not have got a great redundancy deal, the good news for Máirín was that John Mulcahy was not finished with newspapers and nor, as a result, was she.

---

393 Padraig Yeates interview

16. Journalism Mark Two: The Sunday Tribune

After the demise of *Hibernia* in 1980, Mulcahy, with the support of businessman Hughie McLaughlin, started a new paper, *The Sunday Tribune*. Máirín and some colleagues transferred to the *Tribune* where the first editor was Conor Brady, who later went on to edit *The Irish Times*. Máirín was a general news reporter and her first few articles covered topics such as compensation for Garda next of kin, the closure of Pierce's foundry in Wexford, a report on opposition to a new Courts Bill and a row about the non-appearance of women's liberation activist, Betty Friedan, on *The Late Late Show*.[394]

However, Máirín was able also to return to the issues she had campaigned on and had written about in *Hibernia* - women's rights, inequality and poverty.

---

394 *The Sunday Tribune, 2nd-30th November 1980*

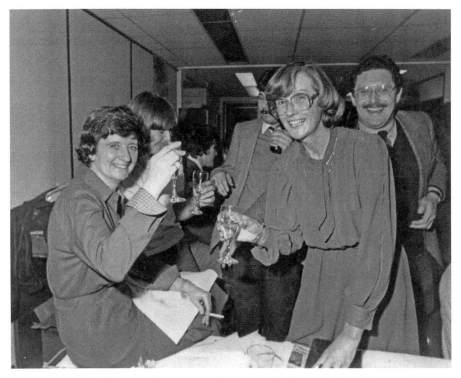

Máirín and her colleagues celebrate the launch of The Sunday Tribune in 1980. De Burca archive.

Abortion Trek

For Irish women and anyone with a progressive view of the world, the 1980s in Ireland was a depressing decade. Issues such as abortion and divorce were subjects of public and political debate and there was huge opposition to their introduction into 'Catholic Ireland'.

At the beginning of 1981 Máirín wrote about the 'abortion trek' so many women made to Britain and the legal loophole which appeared to allow organisations give information on services available 'across the water'.[395] This issue surfaced regularly in Máirín's articles and in March 1981 she reviewed the work of Cura, the Catholic church sponsored counselling organisation for pregnant women.

Her article questioned whether Cura was in fact 'encouraging' women to pursue adoption. Anne Connolly from the Well Woman Centre was quoted as suggesting that Cura "from what our clients tell us, outline the effects of an abortion in a way that leaves the young pregnant woman in more distress and confusion."[396] Articles such as these challenged Máirín's objectivity and occasionally, via her questioning, her point of view slipped into her journalism.

Máirín, in her private life, advocated on the abortion issue. In the run up to the 1981 General Election, along with some prominent feminists, she set up the 'Women's Ad Hoc Election Committee'. This group called for the decriminalisation of abortion and the introduction of divorce. Máirín noted that "no woman candidate, feminist or otherwise, from either of the two major parties has come out in favour of civil divorce."[397] Given she was also writing about these issues as a journalist, Máirín was walking a fine line revealing her personal views in this way.

---

395 *The Sunday Tribune,* 4th January 1981
396 *The Sunday Tribune,* 15th March 1981
397 *The Irish Times,* 5th May 1981

Máirín was writing within an environment of huge public and political debate on the abortion issue. A powerful 'pro-life' lobby had emerged which feared the introduction of abortion and sought to have the constitution changed so that the 'right to life' would be copper fastened.

Máirín wrote about the work of the Pro-Life Amendment Campaign (PLAC) which pushed hard for a referendum. They had a clear, simple message "pregnancy occurs at fertilisation and any interference after that is murder."[398] Máirín was able to point out that changing the law and/or constitution was anything but simple. She teased out the difficulties in coming up with a wording for any amendment which would not have other, unforeseen consequences. As it transpired, she was dead right.

In 1983, with cross- party political support, the eighth amendment to the constitution was passed which introduced a new article recognising the right to life of the unborn. The article read:

'The State acknowledges the right to life of the unborn and, with due regard to the equal right to life of the mother, guarantees in its laws to respect, and, as far as practicable, by its laws to defend and vindicate that right.

---

398 *The Sunday Tribune*, 3rd May 1981

Over 66% of the voters were in favour. However, this was far from the end of it and the whole sorry affair dragged on, with a number of further constitutional changes, for the next twenty-five years. In 1992 following a particular tragic case involving a pregnant fourteen-year-old girl, which became known as 'the X case', a constitutional amendment was proposed which would allow abortion on grounds of a risk to a woman's health, but which excluded suicide as such a risk. It was defeated. Other amendments were approved which allowed the provision of information on abortion in the State and confirmed the 'right to travel.' In other words', women could be told what was available 'across the water' and they could go there for abortions if they wanted. Just not in Ireland.

Divorce

Another major social and women's issue in the 1980s was divorce. When Máirín joined *The Tribune* the issue was a live one with progressive groups pushing for constitutional change. In an article she wrote which mixed reporting and opinion, Máirín examined one of the key arguments against divorce - that children would end up being damaged as a result. She suggested that couples who couldn't divorce were forced to endure "the unendurable, resolutely turning their faces from what might be a happier existence with someone else and providing a peaceful and loving atmosphere in which the children could grow up."[399]

Máirín suggested that if divorce was allowed children would benefit and adapt to a new arrangement and that divorce would be good for their emotional welfare. Her arguments made a lot of sense, but she was in a minority. The divorce debate rumbled on through the first half of the 1980s and in 1986 a referendum on the issue saw the introduction of divorce being rejected by the Irish people, 63% to 36%. It was to be a further decade until divorce was approved in the 1995 referendum.

General Election

Another general election was held in June 1981 and both before and after the election Máirín wrote about one of her regular topics - women in politics. She was quite prepared to acknowledge the good work of any female politician, no matter what party they represented. Shortly before the election, in a review of the women TDs in the Dáil, Máirín wrote that Fianna Fail Minister, Máire Geoghegan Quinn, had "done her ministerial job as well, if not better, than any man in Fianna Fail. She is an intelligent, capable woman, self-assured and vital."[400]

However, Máirín went on to point out that none of the women TDs were prepared to challenge their party's

---

399 *The Sunday Tribune*, 22nd February 1981
400 *The Sunday Tribune*, 31st May 1981

policies on women's issues and suggested that "the failure of women at successive elections is precisely because their sisters cannot tell their political principles apart from those of their male colleagues."[401] A harsh assessment for the small handful of women amongst over one hundred men in the Dáil, but Máirín was not in the business of handing out bouquets.

Before the election Máirín also questioned Fine Gael on its women's policies. In response she got a large helping of waffle and confusion. She concluded that the party had no policy on divorce and forced party leader Garret Fitzgerald to admit the party was 'divided on the matter'. Fitzgerald refused to tell Máirín whether Fine Gael was in favour of contraception for all.[402]

By the end of 1981, her first year in *The Tribune*, Máirín was a frustrated woman and that shone through in an end of year article she wrote looking at the situation of women. Its headline was 'Promises, promises and more damned promises' which aptly summarised her viewpoint. She reviewed all the main parties' election promises and what had happened since then. Her answer? "Well, to put it succinctly – damn little... The women's prison ... goes full steam ahead, there has been no sign of legislation on rape, family planning, domicile or property rights."[403]

---

401 Ibid.
402 *The Sunday Tribune*, 12th April 1981
403 *The Sunday Tribune*, 27th December 1981

It was depressingly familiar, and it was hard to take much comfort from the recent election results, with the new Dáil having just eleven women TDs out of one hundred and sixty six. Rather optimistically Máirín suggested that if they acted together "the female TDs could achieve a great deal for women, whether as mothers, wives, the victims of violence or the sole support of aged and incapacitated parents."[404] Both she and her readers would have been right not to hold their breaths.

Women's Equality

In her time with *The Tribune* Máirín was given opportunities to write about women and equality, opportunities she took with relish. Early in her career with the paper she set out her stall and wrote that "the Irish women's movement has been the greatest success story of the last decade."[405] No undue modesty there, although Máirín was referring to the totality of effort made by women, individually and collectively.

She suggested this success happened despite "male and - it must be admitted - some female opposition, despite the almost universal antagonism and contempt of the media and despite government attempts to pretend that if they ignored it the demands for equality legislation would go away."[406] When Máirín was in full flow no one was safe, including her colleagues in the media.

---

404 ibid
405 *The Sunday Tribune,* 8th March 1981
406 Ibid

Throughout her career Máirín had campaigned for equality in the workplace for women. Although she wasn't campaigning as such while a journalist, she focused on the issue whenever she could. In March 1981 a report on 'Women in Broadcasting' saw her looking at the position of women in RTE. One of her interviewees, producer Tish Barry, told Máirín that "There are still men in technical line management who think women should be home cooking and minding the children."[407] Máirín noted that there had been some improvements in RTE but still there were only three women in top management positions and just sixteen of one hundred and sixteen editorial positions were held by women.[408] It really was a long and winding road.

The ending of the 'marriage bar', where women had to resign their civil service jobs upon marriage, finally came about in 1973. It was supposed to bring about great opportunities for women but Máirín turned her sceptical eye on developments in the civil service. In June 1981, eight years after the bar was ended, she reported that there were only twelve women in the three highest grades. It was a case of equality, but not just yet.

Over in the semi state organisations (ESB, Aer Lingus, IDA) it wasn't much better. In 1981 just 7% of management/professional jobs in the ESB were held by women. Máirín was told by the company that positive

---

407 *The Sunday Tribune*, 19th April 1981
408 ibid

discrimination wasn't an option as "the men employees would resent it."[409] Part of the problem was that girls weren't able to study science subjects in school and then couldn't progress into the more technical and better paid positions. They ended up in what Máirín described as the 'dead end jobs' with low pay.

However, Máirín was not despairing and noted that women were changing. "Increasingly women were buying their own homes. Many are beginning to see singleness as a positive choice and are accepting at a relatively early age that they may always be financially self -dependent whatever their sexual relations."[410] What's more, many women were also driving cars. To twenty first century eyes all this must seem quaint and bizarre, but in 1980s Ireland these were the grim realities women faced.

By the time Máirín got to Aer Lingus, the third of her semi-states, she must have been rightly fed up. The same statistics, the same barriers and the same excuses. Just one woman in the top three management grades and other women confined to being 'cailín fáiltes', presumably to welcome male VIPs. Máirín was told that "When they ceased to be 'cailíns' they got a gentle tap on the shoulder and found themselves with backroom jobs."[411]

Máirín's review of women in the workplace in 1981 was a depressing litany. She must have wondered how far

---

409 *The Sunday Tribune*, 18th August 1981
410 Ibid
411 *The Sunday Tribune*, 30th August 1981

women had come since she started working herself thirty years earlier. But her writing had shone a spotlight on an area badly in need of reform, and that did come, albeit many years later

Light Relief

Amidst all the serious stuff, there were occasions when Máirín could write about lighter matters. In the summer of 1981 she wrote about the removal of chest measurement criteria for Garda recruits. Given it was the 'silly season' Máirín went to town on the issue. Noting that in her eyes guards were getting younger, she wrote, "You can tell they are uncomfortable in their first pair of long trousers, and you mind your tongue when you speak to them for fear they might be shocked or burst into tears or start sucking their thumbs."[412]

This was not a woman who was going to easily forgive and forget. Máirín went on to recount a story from her postering days when a young guard approached her and said she was under arrest. "Then his voice cracked in the middle of the sentence - it did, I swear it did - I laughed and told him to leave me alone and nearly fell off the footpath when he did."[413]

Máirín wrote that 'she felt guilty ever since' but it didn't stop her continuing to poke fun, writing that she blamed "the whole thing on Woman's Lib…. Ever since they took

---

412 *The Sunday Tribune*, 23rd August 1981
413 ibid

in the Ban Gardaí (female guards) the whole force has being going steadily downhill. They have been giving the men ferocious inferiority complexes."[414] When it came to the guards Máirín's commentary was always laced with a few barbs.

Anything for a story. A worried looking Máirín pets a tiger cub as part of a report for the paper. Clearly not her type of cat. c.1981. De Burca archive

Another opportunity for light relief surfaced in July 1981 when Máirín was sent to review the opening of David Marshall's hair salon in Dublin's Dawson Street. From the outset Máirín made her attitude clear when she admitted to "sometimes, mostly, cutting my own hair by means of two mirrors and a nail scissors."[415] After sending the whole venture up she couldn't resist being serious. "You

414 Ibid
415 *The Sunday Tribune*, 12th July 1981

may consider it all part of the great male con job on women. They (these hairdressers) leave impressionable young women with the notion that if they don't conform to what they have decreed as the latest fashion, they might as well stick their heads in the gas oven and be done with it. Some day we will tell them all to go to hell."[416]

Redundant Again

This new Sunday paper was lively and vibrant and quickly built up a substantial readership. Finances, however, were a constant problem and these difficulties were exacerbated when the owners launched a new daily newspaper. It lasted less than a month, drained the company's finances and by October 1982 *The Tribune* had folded. For the second time in two years Máirín was made redundant.

Redundancy gave Máirín the opportunity to do the odd article for *Magill* magazine, including one on her old IWLM colleague Nuala Fennell who in 1983 was a TD and Minister of State for Women's Affairs. Fennell had invited a large number of female journalists into the Dáil to discuss women's issues but Máirín was not impressed and made that clear in her article. In response to a question from Mary Maher on the Minister's input into that year's budget Máirín surmised that the answer was 'none'. She went on to write that "it was on the question

416 ibid

of divorce that prevarication was raised to an art form", with Fennell in favour of an 'all party committee' to consider the matter but refusing to repeat her own personal support for the introduction of divorce.[417]

On the controversial issue of the abortion referendum, Fennell told the journalists she was in favour of the amendment and when challenged by Nell Mc Cafferty if she supported the continuation of all pregnancies even those resulting from rape and incest Fennell's response was 'I don't understand the question.'

Máirín wrote that "It all went downhill from there… She (Nuala Fennell) didn't believe that the amendment, if passed, would make any difference and the reason she supported it in that case was because it was a party pledge. At this point even the experienced political women in the audience were momentarily speechless."[418]

New Editor

In 1983 long established journalist and former *Magill* editor Vincent Browne stepped in to buy *The Tribune* and it was soon back on the streets with Browne himself as editor. Part of the arrangement with the NUJ in the relaunched paper was that Browne agreed to take on any of the old *Tribune* staff who wanted to join. Máirín felt 'This was like a red rag to a bull. He had to take on four

417 *'No Minister'* - *Magill Magazine*, March 1983
418 Ibid.

or five of us. He spent the whole time trying to get rid of us'.

Despite this view, Vincent Browne thought highly of Máirín as a campaigner for social justice. He also considered that her experience as a journalist was meagre. Browne does not believe he was uncomfortable taking Máirín on and regarded her as a 'quiet presence' in the office. He recalls that his contact with Máirín was minimal.[419]

Pat Brennan joined *The Tribune* as news editor in 1985. She was Máirín's direct 'boss' although she is quick to point out that "Máirín did not have a boss, never had a boss and never will have a boss and that's part of the wonder of her."[420]

Brennan had known Máirín from the political scene in Dublin but now had the challenging job of getting the best out of her. Like her relationship with John Mulcahy, Máirín was capable of saying no to Brennan when asked to do a particular story or to make it so difficult Brennan would have to turn to someone else. "She wouldn't do anything she found appalling, such as interviewing the family of someone bereaved." Brennan considered Máirín to be a good writer and she was often given social affairs to cover, although she was also comfortable writing 'fluffy' articles on animals and gardens.[421]

---

419 Vincent Browne interview
420 Pat Brennan interview
421 ibid

As Ireland's depressing decade unfolded, Máirín continued to write about social issues of concern to women and her articles are a telling commentary on the inadequacy of support services in this area. At the end of 1984 she reported on the setting up of the first sexual assault treatment centre in Dublin's Rotunda hospital. It was a big step forward, as before this rape victims had to be examined by a Garda doctor who was usually male.[422] At that time Máirín reported also that the Rape Crisis Centre in Dublin had just one full time counsellor for their clients.[423] A couple of weeks later she was writing about the experiences of women and children who had spent Christmas in a hostel for what was then called 'battered wives.' One of the staff told Máirín that they could only afford to have the heating on for two hours in the morning and two at night. Máirín painted a grim picture of a grim time.[424]

The delicate nature of all matters to do with contraception was vividly illustrated when then Health Minister Barry Desmond introduced a Family Planning Bill in 1985 which was to legalise the sale of contraceptives to people over the age of eighteen. This move caused intense debate and opposition across the country. Máirín reported that the Single Women's Association and the Federation of Women's clubs had resigned from the Council for the Status of Women over the issue.[425] Desmond's Bill was

---

422 *The Sunday Tribune, 9th December 1984*
423 *The Sunday Tribune,* 13th January 1985
424 *The Sunday Tribune,* 6th January 1985
425 *The Sunday Tribune, 3rd* March 1985

eventually enacted and the country moved another small step towards becoming a modern society.

It wasn't always about women and in January 1985 Máirín had a front-page story where she reported on the existence of the 'Prisoners' Revenge Group', an extraordinary name for a group of former prisoners, which had attacked and injured four prison officers and had plans to also attack their families. The group claimed their action was in retaliation for assaults by prison officers.[426] The creation of such a group sounded and was very disturbing and indicated the dire state of relations within a prison system which Máirín had campaigned to change over many years.

Máirín's front page story on the Prisoners' Revenge Group.1985.

Máirín continued to have the occasional opportunity to write about lighter issues.As a dog lover she must have been pleased to be sent to report on the Crufts annual dog show, the World Cup of the canine world. Máirín

---

426 *The Sunday Tribune*, 13th January 1985

was told that it would cost between £3000-4000 (about £11,500 in 2023) to compete at the top levels in the show, so this wasn't for the ordinary punter. She was also amused to learn that the Chinese Crested breed, almost completely hairless, was used by Chinese people as a bed warmer.[427] An interesting idea to share with her readers.

Office Eruption

Despite her 'quiet presence', Máirín recalls one instance when Browne 'erupted in the office, pointed at me and shouted - you're sacked.' Máirín went to the father of the union chapel who told her to let it calm down, which it did. Máirín was told there was a procedure to go through which would take two years, but the issue was never mentioned again. Vincent Browne is "100% certain" that he never said any such thing, not even as a joke. He is very clear that "I wouldn't do that to anybody."[428] While she didn't witness this incident, Pat Brennan knew that "Vincent could say outrageous things that wouldn't last a day."[429]

Coincidentally, Máirín's colleague from her DHAC days, Eamonn Farrell, ended up working in *The Tribune* as well, becoming its pictures editor. They worked on some assignments together but generally photographers and reporters operated separately. Farrell also had the

---

427 *The Sunday Tribune,* 14th February 1985
428 Vincent Browne interview
429 Pat Brennan interview

occasional 'run in' with the editor and eventually moved on.

Máirín and friends on a day out. c.1983. L to R Maura Friel, Britta Smith, Máirín, Evelyn Roden. De Burca archive.

Working for a newspaper can be hectic and stressful. There are deadlines to be met and egos to be massaged. Under these pressures nerves can get frayed. Máirín was always good at meeting deadlines. She was older than a lot of her colleagues and she didn't need to prove herself like some of the younger journalists. Because of her political and campaigning exploits, her colleagues had huge respect for her. This was a woman who had 'walked the walk' and was never shy of saying exactly what she thought. She was also someone who was supportive of colleagues, especially women or those who were getting a hard time.[430] Máirín also made sure that the job didn't consume her as Sinn Fein had done. She made time for her friends, for outings and other social activities.

Mercurial Boss

Vincent Browne could rightly be described as one of the best Irish journalists of the last fifty years. Across various outlets – *Magill, The Irish Press, The Irish Times, The Sunday Tribune* and *TV3* to name just a few - he had an impressive track record of pioneering current affairs journalism with an important input on social issues. His colleague in the *Tribune* Pat Brennan describes him as a "great journalist" but also someone who was "mercurial, when he is good he is very, very good and when he is bad, he is horrid."[431] Browne's great enthusiasm for his work did not always sit easily with Máirín's calmer approach and sometimes she poured cold water on his ideas.

Máirín regarded her editor as difficult. 'We didn't get on as a boss and worker. He was demanding and never happy. Others got on with him, I didn't… If I met him now, we would probably be the best of pals.' Browne was interested in long detailed, articles and that type of journalism was not Máirín's strength. 'He was always at me to do an article on the Irish language; he was brought up speaking Irish, but he couldn't get his head around the state promoting it.' Máirín made a number of visits to the Department of Education to try and establish how

---

430 Pat Brennan interview
431 ibid

304

much money the state was spending on educating people in the language but failed to come up with final figures. However, 'Vincent wouldn't accept that. He simply wouldn't. I did the article and redid it and did it again. Eventually, I told him I couldn't do it. This article is not going to be done by me.'

For his part Browne says, "It is wrong to suggest I was against the Irish language or saw it as wasting money. I wasn't in favour of it being compulsory. I used to speak it fluently myself and I am a believer in it. I don't recall asking Máirín to pursue that story."[432]

As the saying goes there were two of them in it and Máirín would acknowledge that 'With Vincent and myself you had two forceful personalities and I'm not good at taking orders. If something doesn't appeal to my rational side, I won't do it.'

Despite these difficulties Máirín continued to write about social affairs and women's issues. In September 1985 she wrote about striking women cleaners in UCD[433] and the following year she was highlighting the appointment of a new chief officer, Anne Good, in the Council for the Status of Women, an organisation beset by internal difficulties,[434] something with which Máirín was very familiar.

There was also an opportunity before the end of 1985 to acknowledge the commitment of the small, mainly

---

432 Vincent Browne interview
433 *The Sunday Tribune*, 8th September 1985
434 *The Sunday Tribune*, 13th October 1985

female, group of Dunne's stores workers who had gone on strike in protest against selling South African goods. The strike had been running for seventeen months and the worker's union had decided to suspend the strike as the government had decided to investigate whether prison labour had been used to produce goods on sale in Ireland. If that was the case the government could move to ban them.

Despite the length of their strike, some of the strikers told Máirín they were unhappy with the decision. One told her "It would keep the dispute in people's minds and keep the pressure on the government." Mary Manning, the woman whose refusal to sell South African goods started the strike, had no regrets. She told Máirín "I would do it all again-every single day of it."[435] In the end the strikers perseverance paid off and in March 1986 the government announced that they would introduce a ban on South African produce.

Labour Pains

Understandably, Máirín was not asked to write about politics but occasionally she dipped her toe in those murky waters. In December 1985 she was confidently able to report that trade union official and former Communist Party activist, Bernard Browne, was to be appointed the new general secretary of the Labour Party. Browne was also a colleague of Máirín's in the

---

435 *The Sunday Tribune*, 29th December 1985

DHAC and most likely gave her the story. The Labour Party was in a coalition government with Fine Gael at the time and Browne made clear to Máirín that he was "Totally opposed to coalition and that is well known in the party…The party in coalition has lost electoral support and credibility among the workers."[436] Browne went on to tell Máirín that the party's electoral strategy on employment and taxation had failed.

The article appeared on a Sunday and by the following Tuesday the appointment was anything but secure. The party's ruling body had a row over the issue, with party leader Dick Spring against the appointment and party chairman, Michael D. Higgins, in favour. Eventually the party deferred making an immediate decision and by the following January Browne was gone and a more acceptable candidate took his place. It was the interview with Máirín that ended Bernard Browne's chances, but he really should have known better.

There were times as a journalist when Máirín must have had to bite her tongue. Early in 1986 British Labour Party MP, Claire Short, sought to introduce legislation banning the display of partly naked women in newspapers - the Page Three phenomenon. Máirín conducted a brief vox pop on the issue with one man telling her that the page three pin ups "cheer me up in the morning."[437] This man obviously had no idea about Máirín's feminist pedigree.

436 *The Sunday Tribune*, 1st December 1985
437 *The Sunday Tribune*, 16th February 1986

"The Labour Party in coalition has lost electoral support"

MÁIRÍN DE BURCA talks to Labour's next general secretary

BERNARD BROWNE will be confirmed as the new general secretary of the Labour Party when the party's Administrative Council meets next Tuesday. housing in the city and, of course, eventually we had to leave. So we squatted in empty private property in Mountjoy Square. We got a bad time from the landlord coalition and this is well known in the party and to the interview committee. The party in coalition has lost electoral support and credibility amongst the

Máirín's scoop on Bernard Browne and the appointment that wasn't. 1985

Whenever Máirín wrote about 'women's issues', the issue of contraception was rarely far away. Barry Desmond's Family Planning Act came into effect in 1985 but by the following year progress in the provision of support services was very slow. Máirín reported on the setting up of a new family planning clinic in the large Dublin suburb of Finglas. The clinic had a quiet start and Máirín was told that "All the customers so far have been women and the pill is still the favourite form of contraception with them."[438] The article suggested it was no coincidence that this new service had been set up in the constituency of Worker's Party TD, Proinsias De Rossa. Máirín discovered that most of the country's eight health boards had no plans to provide a family planning service.

---

438 *The Sunday Tribune*, 13th April 1986

Financial Problems

Finances were a constant problem in *The Tribune* and while Browne may have been a good journalist, he was described by news editor Pat Brennan as a "terrible businessman" and there were times when he recruited more staff than he needed.[439] Not what you need when you are trying to survive in the rocky financial world of journalism. At one stage Browne asked staff to accept a pay cut. By then Máirín had moved to a new house in Fairview which carried a substantial mortgage, and reducing her salary was not an option. She wrote down her own personal budget and when she showed it to Browne he didn't force the issue.

Eventually, Máirín was offered a redundancy package and used Browne's desire to hire his own staff as a lever to get the best possible deal. Pat Brennan believes that the deal was reasonable, and that Vincent Browne had no desire to impoverish Máirín.[440] This financial settlement enabled Máirín to clear her mortgage. She was now into her 50s and knew her chances of another full-time job were practically non-existent. Another chapter in her very varied life was about to begin.

---

439 Pat Brennan Interview
440 Ibid.

17. Back To Politics

After Máirín left *The Sunday Tribune* she experienced another period of unemployment and took on various temporary secretarial positions. It wasn't exciting work, but it helped pay the bills. And then, somewhat unexpectedly, and after a gap of over twenty years, she re-entered the world of politics. Only this time she was inside the Dáil gates.

Rabbitte Elected

In 1989 Pat Rabbitte was elected as a TD for the Workers Party in the Dublin South West constituency. Rabbitte had been active in this sprawling constituency, which incorporated Tallaght and Clondalkin, since the early 1980s and had previously been a County Councillor. The demands on a TD in these areas were many and varied. Rabbitte decided that he wanted someone working alongside him who was experienced in politics and likeminded in their political views.[441] He turned to Máirín who he had first encountered in the 1970s during various campaigns when he was President of the Union of Students in Ireland (USI). As a young student activist Rabbitte would have viewed Máirín as "very severe, very assured in her views and possibly sceptical of pampered students. I was probably afraid of her."[442]

---

441 Pat Rabbitte interview
442 ibid

Pat Rabbitte celebrates his election as a TD for the Workers Party in 1989. Courtesy National Photographic Archive and Independent Newspapers Archive.

Despite this and the advice of his colleague, Tony Heffernan, Rabbitte appointed Máirín as his constituency secretary. Heffernan had told Rabbitte that Máirín was the wrong woman for this type of job as he anticipated clashes between two very strong-willed people with definite views.[443] It turned out to be good if unheeded advice.

Given the constituency Rabbitte represented there was a large clientelist dimension to a TDs workload, especially a left-wing TD. A major part of Máirín's job was to handle constituency queries. Máirín was organised and

---

443 Tony Heffernan interview

efficient in her work but found her 'boss' difficult to please. 'I would have his day organised from morning to night… a file on everyone who would ring, all written down and up to date within twenty-four hours. It was never enough. He was always frightened he would lose his seat because of me.' Rabbitte was a very hard worker and in Máirín's eyes, a workaholic who she sometimes told needed to spend more time with his family.

While Máirín was employed as constituency secretary she found it hard not to become more involved than that. In Pat Rabbitte's view "Máirín wasn't opposed to clientelism but with her you sometimes got clientelism with a lecture. She wasn't happy merely to seek to establish the assistance sought. The client very often got an earful about the fundamental causes of her plight."[444] So, in an instance where a woman rang complaining that her husband had spent all the money on drink, the woman might get a lecture on what to do about the husband.

On one particular occasion a mother with eleven children, two of them intellectually disabled, phoned in. "She probably struggled to get a phone box that worked and maybe spent her last 20 pence phoning me. When she explained her situation, part of Máirín's response was ' Have you never heard of contraception out there.' That led to an interesting discussion afterwards."[445]

Máirín was a woman with her own very definite views and as her former 'boss' suggests, a better role for her

---

444 Pat Rabbitte interview'
445 Ibid

would have been as a TD where she would have an ideal platform for her opinions. For her part Máirín, despite running for election on a couple of occasions, was very sure that she wasn't cut out for political life. Her experience with Pat Rabbitte confirmed her thinking about the job of a TD. 'Quite frankly I don't think they get paid enough. The work they do, and again it's never enough. Once you become a TD your life is not yours. I don't know why anyone wants to do it.'

Máirín's tenure as secretary to Rabbitte unwound after about eighteen months and she moved on. Before leaving she did have the opportunity to enter one of the elite bastions of Leinster House. Looking for her TD one day she was told that he was in the Members' Bar. On being told the bar was strictly for 'members', Máirín marched down and strode into the bar, shocking all those present. It probably didn't help her relationship with her 'boss'.

Notwithstanding any tensions between Máirín and Pat Rabbitte, her former employer is fulsome in his praise. "She's a remarkable woman. A once off and extraordinarily strong minded. She was determined to make a difference."[446]

Pussy Cat Proinsias

After Pat Rabbitte, Máirín remained within Leinster House and worked for a short period for Proinsias De

---

446 ibid

Rossa, then both a TD and Member of the European Parliament (MEP). Máirín regarded De Rossa as a 'pussycat' (what then was Deputy Rabbitte?) who let her get on with the work. 'He was one of those guys who let you get on with it. He knew me well enough to know that I would treat his constituents well and would know what to do.'

The work with De Rossa was varied and interesting. Máirín helped arrange some of his schedule and deal with the long stream of constituency queries, where housing was always top of the list. Relations were built up with civil servants and local authority officials and by and large Máirín found these people reasonable to work with. There were, of course, the regular callers. One woman would ring every Monday morning complaining that her windows had been broken over the weekend. After Dublin Corporation replaced the windows on a couple of occasions, they told Máirín the culprits were the woman's two sons who went on a drunken spree every weekend.

And there was the woman who, with the 'help' of a son with credit card debts, owed rent of €3,000. She rang De Rossa's office one Friday evening and Máirín urged her to get a credit union loan and make sure her husband was part of the application. The following Monday she rang again. 'Did you tell your husband? No. Why not? The World Cup matches were on, and I didn't want to spoil it for him.' How Máirín responded is not known but she never heard from that particular constituent again.

Proinsias De Rossa's election poster for the 1989 European elections. De Rossa was comfortably elected. Tony Heffernan archive, UCD archives.

After De Rossa gave up the 'dual mandate' and resigned as an MEP, Máirín worked briefly for his replacement, Des Geraghty, her former DHAC colleague and by then an established trade union and political activist. Geraghty had spent his career working for the Irish Transport and General Workers Union (ITGWU) and its successor the Services Industry Professional and Technical Union (SIPTU). He was also a member of the Workers Party and was an obvious successor to De Rossa.

Máirín was based in a party office in Dublin's Abbey Street but her time working for Geraghty didn't last too long. In any event when the European elections came round in 1994 Geraghty decided not to run. The world had moved on and so had Máirín. By this time she was in her mid-fifties and wanted to give up full time work. She had been working in different jobs for forty years and it was time to step back. Her formal involvement in the political world had come to an end but her life of activism continued.

18. Working In The Community

While Máirín's full time working career was over she still needed and wanted to be active and useful. Máirín was always a worker and quite prepared to turn her hand to anything. After forty years of full-time work, she wanted something which was interesting, part time and brought in some money. Working as a home help fulfilled those requirements. 'I was very badly paid, but you got cash once a month and it paid a couple of bills. You also felt useful, keeping the clients in their homes where they wanted to be'. Máirín supplemented her home help work with various temporary secretarial positions. Whether she had to wear skirts is not known.

Not just a cat lover. Máirín at home with her dog Isolde. c. 2001.
De Burca archive.

Credit Union

As she was no longer working full time, Máirín had time for more community-based activities. She had joined her local credit union in Fairview in1984 and stayed involved until 2021. Like everything else she did, she threw herself into the work and at different times she served as secretary, chairperson and loans officer. And probably washed the floors if they needed it. This was a woman with no 'notions' whatsoever and who certainly didn't like to see them in others.[447]

Being involved in a credit union gave Máirín a good insight into the economic and social 'state of play' of the community it serves. In Fairview, where many of the houses were of a certain age, a lot of borrowings were for home improvements. Bad debts were few as the customers were known to the staff. Changes in the way the Movement operates did not impress Máirín. 'People respected their credit union. We knew our customers but that's all going now as we get bigger…. We merged with another credit union and they don't use volunteers. The Central Bank wanted us to coalesce; they wanted us to become a bank. It's not the same as when I joined. You felt you were contributing to the local community.' At a personal level Máirín acknowledged that "The credit union movement kept my house upright when I wouldn't have had a lot of money."[448]

447 Pat Brennan interview
448 The Better Side Podcast

Máirín at her desk in Fairview Credit Union. c.2000.
De Burca archive.

Most Powerful Man

Máirín wrote the occasional article as a freelance journalist and in 1988 her subject was Gay Byrne's radio show. He was, as the headline suggested, 'The Most Powerful Man in Ireland'. And this time her former editor in *Hibernia*, John Mulcahy, wasn't there to stop her. Byrne's morning radio programme was a broadcasting phenomenon. It combined social welfare and consumer advice with opportunities for listeners to come on air and talk about whatever was on their mind. Over time it became a large community confessional.

Máirín described 'Gaybo' as "by turns light hearted and serious, soothing and cross but rarely putting a foot or a word wrong and inducing people - mainly women - to open their hearts and their lives for his and our inspection."[449] Máirín's former colleague in the IWLM, June Levine, worked as a researcher on the programme. She recognised Byrne's rapport with women. "He is nearly always on their side and if you combine that with the desperate isolation of many women in the home and their need at times for an intelligent adult voice completely attentive to them... there is almost a compulsion to ring him up and unburden themselves."[450] Byrne himself suggested that "there are an awful lot of nice intelligent women who are streets ahead of the lumps they are married to."[451]

Although it was 'only' a radio programme, the Gay Byrne show really was a social phenomenon and its success was well worth exploring. Máirín put most of it down to the uncanny ability of the man himself to "reach into people's minds and hearts, with little effort persuading them to open up to him and a million or so other people... For many isolated women he clearly provides a safety valve."[452] It was over twenty years since the IWLM was set up, but this radio programme made clear Irish women were still far from being liberated.

---

449 *Irish Examiner*, 15th November 1988
450 Ibid.
451 ibid
452 ibid

In addition to her occasional journalism and community activities Máirín remained involved in her various 'causes'. She remained involved with the PRO until it faded away and continued to be active on the Palestine issue. These were lifelong commitments.

Mr. Nabil Ramlawi, PLO representative in London, with Máirín at a reception held by the Irish Friends of Palestine in the Shelbourne Hotel, Dublin. 1981. Photograph: Jimmy McCormack. THE IRISH TIMES.

19. Grand Dame Of The Left

At a certain stage in her life, when the battles and the bottle throwing, the fights and the flag burning, had all faded into a romanticised past, Máirín moved on to become something of a 'Grand Dame of the Left'. If, that is, 'the Left' in Ireland would tolerate such a thing. She was invited onto podcasts to talk about her career; there was a sculpture made in her honour; she was awarded an honorary degree and she was even invited to engage with the prison system. Despite being feted, Máirín never lost her edge and continued to speak out or challenge as she saw fit.

Prison Visitor

Máirín's interest in the operation of the prison system remained a constant in her life. In 1995 her name was put forward by then government minister Proinsias De Rossa for appointment to a prison visiting committee. The function of these committees still remained that of visiting prisons and hearing any complaints prisoners might have. Their membership came from a cross section of society and each committee prepared an annual report on whichever prison they visited. The Prisoners' Rights Organisation had found them somewhat toothless, and their annual reports weren't always readily available, but Máirín was interested.

The great and the good gather to celebrate Máirín's 70th birthday in 2008. Among those in attendance were, Mrs. Gaj, Nell McCafferty, Pat Rabbitte, Eamon Gilmore, Tony Heffernan, Joe Costello, Pat McCartan, Pat Brennan, Máirín Johnston, Moira Woods, Mary Sheerin and Rosita Sweetman. Photo: Derek Speirs.

Luckily for Máirín, neither Gerry Collins nor Des O'Malley was still Minister for Justice. But when she submitted her CV to the Department of Justice one civil servant, referring to the possibility of Máirín joining the Mountjoy jail committee, wrote at the bottom her CV that "we would have to recommend against it. Ms. De Burca has the ability to make life very difficult for the Minister."[453]

The new Minister, Fine Gael's Nora Owen, didn't assign Máirín to Mountjoy and instead appointed her to the visiting committee for Shanganagh Castle, a prison for young offenders. While accepting the appointment Máirín wrote to Nora Owen pointing out she was "assigned to Shanganagh Castle probably the prison furthest from Fairview (where she lived)." She asked for travel expenses and said she planned to visit the prison twice a month, "once for the monthly meeting and once on a spot check to talk to the boys." She concluded her letter by stating that "it is important that at least one person on each Prison Visiting Committee is of the same class and from much the same part of the city as the prisoners. If I am forced to resign…. the Visiting Committee will be composed entirely of middle-class people from South Dublin."[454]

---

453 De Burca archive, no date.
454 Letter to Nora Owen TD, 14th February 1996. De Burca archive

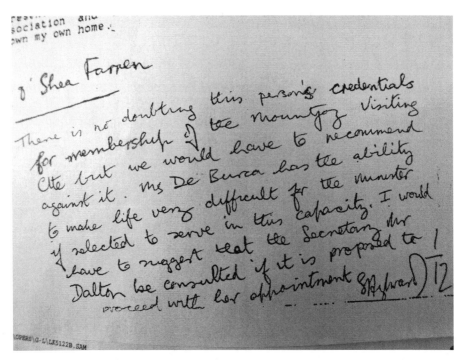

Civil Service advice on Máirín's appointment to a prisoner Visiting Committee.1995. De Burca archive.

Máirín was given her travel expenses and made clear that if she was doing this 'job' she wanted to do it properly. She found it to be a positive experience. 'Although we had all been nominated by different parties, I can truly say there was no conflict. All my co-visitors were determined to see the best done for the young lads.' The Committee had opportunities to meet the young prisoners in private, but any complaints were minor. Máirín believed that during her membership there was never 'any mistreatment… and I found the staff responded well to our submissions. It wasn't a prison for hard guys - none in for drugs or violence.'

After a year in the role Máirín became the Visiting Committee chairperson. But a year after that there was a change of government and John O'Donoghue from Fianna Fail was the new Minister. In December 1997 his private secretary wrote to Máirín to convey the Minister's "sincere appreciation of your valuable past service as a member of the Visiting Committee to Shanganagh Castle Open Centre."[455] The key word in that letter was 'past' and Máirín was never reappointed.

Appeal to Ruairí

Máirín maintained her keen interest in politics and like most people in the country, she watched the development of the 'Good Friday ' agreement in the North with great interest. Coming up to the conclusion of negotiations on the agreement, she wrote to her old Sinn Féin colleague, later adversary, Ruairí Ó Brádaigh, asking him to use only peaceful and constitutional means if he was going to oppose the deal. It was an impassioned appeal. In her letter she wrote "I have … learned … over the past twenty-five years the utter futility of and devastation caused by physical violence used for political ends… Over three thousand people have died violently…and for what? Nothing that could not have been achieved if people had been prepared for the long haul, the road of negotiation and agitation and, yes, compromise."[456]

---

455 Letter from John O'Donoghue, 4th December 1998. De Burca archive.
456 Letter to Ruairí O' Brádaigh, 6th April 1998. De Burca archive.

This letter summed up all Máirín's deep rooted pacifism which she embraced after her youthful flirtation with the physical force approach. In ending her letter, she appealed to Ó'Brádaigh, "I plead with you Ruairí, stop and think before you go further down the road with violence. No intelligent person can see a settlement in the simplistic slogan 'Brits Out'.[457] Ó Brádaigh didn't reply to Máirín's letter, but the Good Friday agreement was concluded four days later and, at last, there was some degree of settlement in the North.

Letter Writer

Through most of her career, Máirín was a regular letter writer to the newspapers. *The Irish Times* was her paper of choice and through the 2000s she continued to give her opinions on a variety of subjects. In 2002 she focused on the behaviour of young people at a recent 'Reclaim the Streets' rally. She noted that young people are often criticised for anti-social behaviour and wrote that "In the area where I live, a green space where I walk my dogs is littered most mornings with their debris - lager cans, vodka bottles ... and other less salubrious evidence of their activities."[458]

Having made that point, Máirín went on to praise the young people at the rally. "Not a picture of perfection -

---

458 ibid
458 *The Irish Times*, 11th May 2002

heaven forbid - but a section of young people who care about the environment, about the poor... and are willing to stand up and say so."[459] Then, almost inevitably, the guards who marshalled the rally got a tongue lashing. "And the Gardai, which spends much of its time ... complaining about anti-social activities ranging from vandalism to murder, beat the hell out of them."[460]

Máirín rarely commented publicly about young people and it is possible that her experience of the Shanganagh Castle Visiting Committee prompted her to write about them. The letter shows her usual combination of bluntness, compassion and anger at the "activities of the blue shirted ones who behaved like lager louts."[461]

IRA Ceasefire

Other issues which encouraged her to reach for her keyboard, included the IRA's announcement of a permanent ceasefire in 2005. While welcoming this decision Máirín displayed her ongoing anger and demand for answers when she wrote, "It would be a terrible neglect to the memory of the dead if we did not demand of the IRA ... what 3,000 people died for."[462] Once again she asked a question she had put repeatedly

---

459 Ibid
460 ibid
461 Ibid.
462 *The Irish Times*, 30th July 2005

when active in Sinn Féin, "what has been gained that would not have been achieved by political activity?"[463] Máirín, and many more like her, never got a satisfactory answer.

In different letters she railed against what must have seemed to her to be Ireland's never ending housing crisis and the failure of politicians to grasp the nettle of how to raise the necessary finance to build more homes. In 2011 she hit out at "so called socialists threatening to go to jail rather than pay charges for local authority services... Get a grip lads and lassies... If I we're going to jail again it wouldn't be for a little less euro in my pocket, but for the thousands out there with real, immediate and desperate needs."[464]

Six years later she was at it again, advocating the return of rates and suggested, "It is time the Irish taxpayer grew up and accepted the fact that benefits have to be paid for. If we are to have clean water, housing for the poor, regular bin collections etc., it will cost us."[465] Máirín was right about one thing – she really wouldn't have been a very successful politician.

---

463 ibid
464 *The Irish Times*, 17th December 2011
465 *The Irish Times*, 9th September 2017

Information Request

Sometimes it seemed as if Máirín and the Department of Justice couldn't do without each other. A further development in their 'relationship' arose in 2003 and 2004 when Máirín, at the age of sixty six, sought any file or documents the Department held on her, using Freedom of Information legislation to support her request. In response Máirín was sent a number of press cuttings, all of them clearly in the public domain.

Máirín wrote back to the Department stating she couldn't "for the life of me see the risk in releasing the information now. We are not talking major security risks here, what was involved was fairly run of the mill political activism none of it violent, at least on my part." There were those in the Department who would probably dispute the 'run of the mill' phrase but Máirín went on to point out that she was on no "mission to revenge myself on anyone who may have given information to the Gardaí about my activities. Nothing they did resulted in any harm to me or mine and presumably they had their reasons as I had mine."

Máirín concluded her reasoned request by asking that "common sense would surface in the Department of Justice for once and that, before I snuff it, I can see what, in justice, I have a right to see from my file."[466]

---

466 Máirín De Burca- Letter to Dept of Justice, Equality and Law Reform, 5th January 2004, De Burca archive.

Some nineteen years later Máirín De Burca hasn't 'snuffed it' but she is still waiting for information from the Department of Justice. It is interesting to note that she could get a large file from the FBI in Washington and nothing from her own country.

Church Resignation

The series of revelations of child sexual abuse perpetrated by Catholic clergy rocked Irish society in the first decade of the twenty first century. A Commission of Enquiry into this abuse in the Dublin Diocese published its findings in 2009 and its revelations were shocking. In her own small way Máirín decided to respond by 'resigning' from the Catholic church. The process, known formally as 'defection', involved correspondence with the Archdiocese, who pointed out that Máirín's 'defection' meant she could no longer receive sacraments or have a Catholic burial. Máirín had already made her own funeral arrangements so that last prohibition was of no concern to her.

Then Archbishop Diarmuid Martin sent a concerned letter to Máirín about her decision. He wrote " While I fully respect your decision I am always personally saddened when somebody chooses to leave the Church. It causes me to reflect on the reasons and motivations behind such a decision and to wonder if there is something we as a Church can learn from it."[467] Archbishop Martin's letter was clearly heartfelt but Máirín was very clear and comfortable in her decision.

Savita

In October 2012 the death of Savita Halappanavar shocked the country. Savita was a pregnant woman facing an unavoidable miscarriage who was denied an abortion. She developed sepsis and soon afterwards died in hospital. Her death led to widespread protests. Máirín once again, this time with some of her former IWLM colleagues, took to writing to *The Irish Times*

> *Sir, – We know now that Savita Halappanavar died because of clinical failure in hospital. The Dáil is now debating legislation which will ensure that a tiny cohort of women in Ireland will be given the right to terminate a pregnancy which threatens her life. We, the undersigned founder members of the Irishwomen's Liberation Movement, who helped organise the contraceptive train to Belfast in 1971, expect the Dáil to do its duty by these women. Political failure is not an option when a pregnant woman's life is at risk. – Yours, etc,*
>
> *MÁIRÍN de BURCA,*
> *MÁIRÍN JOHNSTON,*
> *MARIE Mac MAHON*
> *NELL Mc CAFFERTY,* [468]

---

467 Diarmuid Martin Letter, 1st June 2010. De Burca archive
468 *The Irish Times*, 21st June 2013

Honorary Degree

Máirín had never been to university but she had given various talks to students in UCD. In 2017 the college came looking for her. They awarded her an honorary degree of Doctor of Laws in recognition of her activism and her successful constitutional challenge of the Juries Act. Máirín was delighted and surprised to be honoured. 'I always wanted the IWLM work to be recognised in some fashion, but I was still gobsmacked when I got the letter from UCD because I expected any recognition to go to someone more respectable.'

The degree was presented by Associate Professor Kevin Costello and UCD President Professor Andrew Feekes. In his address Professor Costello noted that Máirín was a regular speaker at different events in the university since the 1970s. He described Máirín as a "social justice activist and litigant … one of the foremost exemplars of (direct activism) in modern Irish history."[469]

Máirín wore her cap and gown with pride, but the event was a bit of an ordeal. 'I was the only one that day. He had to give a big, long speech and I was so off the wall with nerves I don't remember hearing a thing. A lot of that morning passed in a haze.' Modest as ever, Máirín acknowledged the work of others. 'I know I got the conferral but there is no doubt in my mind that it encompassed the work of the IWLM... in a way it was nice to get the recognition. It tells you that you didn't do any harm.'

---

469 Prof. Kevin Costello, Conferring Address, 5th December 2017, De Burca archive.

Máirín receiving her honorary degree from UCD President,
Professor Andrew Feekes. 2017. De Burca archive

Sculpture

In December 2021 a sculpture called 'The Left Arm of Commerce', by artist Jessie Jones, was unveiled in the King's Inn, the headquarters of barristers in Ireland. The sculpture depicts Máirín holding her copy of the Irish Constitution, Bunreacht na hÉireann. The work was inspired by Máirín and Mary Anderson's role in the Juries Act issue. The sculpture was a creative response to the theme of art and the law.

The evocative and impressive piece emerged from a creative residency programme which Jones undertook, with funding provided by Dublin City Council's Culture Company. Jones had always known about Máirín's activism and in her address at the unveiling she described Máirín as an example of a woman that in breaking the law changed the law. Jones was anxious that her work would meet Máirín's approval. She need not have worried as Máirín described it as "A beautifully realised piece of sculpture. I know that Jesse put her heart and soul into it, and it shows."[470]

This was another positive event for the 'Grand Dame of the Left'. 'Jessie's project was such a joy - surreal but a joy. Like the conferral it brought me into contact with such great people that I would not otherwise have met. Such a bonus when you think that, at your age, that is not going to happen anymore.'

The sculpture remains in Kings Inn as a lasting reminder to what Máirín and Mary Anderson achieved.

470 *The Examiner*, 16th December 2021

Sculptor Jessie Jones and Máirín at the unveiling of
'The Left Arm of Commerce'. Side view of the Sculpture.2021.
Photos. Eamonn Farrell, Rolling News.

Apollo House

In 2016 Máirín, accompanied by her old DHAC colleague Eamonn Farrell, visited Apollo House, an empty office block in the centre of Dublin and the site of a high profile housing occupation cum protest. For both activists, their visit must have brought them back to their many squats such as in Pembroke Road and Gardiner Street. In a letter to *The Irish Times* about Apollo House Máirín wrote

> *Sir, – As a founding member of the old Dublin Housing Action Committee, I applaud the actions of the Home Sweet Home group and others who have taken over Apollo House for the homeless. I am sure that they know quite well, as we did in the 1960s, that this is not a long-term solution but in the short-term it puts a roof over the heads of families. There is absolutely no reason why support is an either-or proposition. It is possible to support the short-term option while fighting fiercely for the basic right of citizens to a permanent secure home. In an era when it seems that only self-interest will bring people out on the streets in protest, it is heartening to see that there are still some who look beyond the cost to themselves and will fight for right and justice for those less privileged. – Yours, etc,*
> *MÁIRÍN de BURCA,*[471]

---

471 *The Irish Times*, 20th December 2016

The Apollo House occupation lasted for a month. The empty office building was renovated and some homeless people moved in and then, on foot of a High Court order, they moved out again. The protest certainly created significant public debate and it did lead to improvements in emergency accommodation for homeless people.

Máirín joins the protest outside the occupied Apollo House in central Dublin. 2016. Photo: Eamonn Farrell, Rolling News.

However, in November 2022, five years after Apollo House and over fifty years after the Dublin Housing Action Committee, there were over 11,500 people in Ireland accessing emergency accommodation. It was a record number, and it must have been depressing for long time campaigners such as Máirín and her other DHAC colleagues to see such grim statistics.

Abortion Referendum

Since the establishment of the IWLM in 1971, a central part of Máirín's concern was a woman's right to make choices about family planning and related matters to do with bodily integrity. Abortion was not a subject that could be discussed easily in the 1970s but as the years rolled on it began to become an issue to be debated.

Máirín had, as a journalist, written about the so called 'Right to Life' abortion referendum in 1983, but once she was finished with journalism she was free to speak out whenever an appropriate opportunity arose. In an interview she gave in 1990 she said, "If a woman wants an abortion, she should be able to get one. I don't think a man has a say in it. I've always felt that. I wouldn't have been able to say that 30 years ago."[472]

Savita Halappanavar's tragic death led to widespread protests and vigils across the country. Demands were made, yet again, for politicians to act. Inevitably, the wheels of change turned slowly and it wasn't until May 2018 that another referendum was held on the issue. The proposed amendment this time was very different to 1983. It read:

---

472 *Evening Press*, 14th November 1990

Provision may be made by law for the regulation of termination of pregnancy.

In other words, if the referendum was passed the Dáil would be allowed to legislate for abortion.

Máirín was an enthusiastic supporter of the referendum and was now able to speak in way she didn't feel able to thirty and forty years ago. Three days before the poll she addressed a meeting organised by the Workers Party. In her contribution she said that "She sincerely hoped this is the last frontier and that women will finally move away from being compelled (to have a baby)."[473]

Thinking back to her IWLM days, Máirín recalled that the Movement then was about two words - choice and equality. "If a woman decides a pregnancy is not for her that's her choice …I have never met a woman who takes such a decision lightly, a woman is more likely to err on the side of keeping her baby." Máirín's address was strong and deeply felt. She said that she disliked the use of the word 'compassion' in the campaign literature. "I wouldn't give you anything for compassion… We are not victims."[474] It was as she said an issue of choice and equality.

This time the Irish electorate voted in favour of the amendment by a large majority. After over forty

473 Máirín De Burca address, Workers Party Meeting, 22nd May 2018
474 Ibid.

years campaigning on the issue of women's rights the outcome gave Máirín considerable satisfaction. In the aftermath of the poll she reacted angrily to one catholic archbishop who claimed that the right to life of the unborn had been 'obliterated'. In another of her newspaper letters Máirín disagreed: "What it is in the process of doing is obliterating the race memory of generations of Irish women who were degraded and enslaved by the Roman Catholic Church in Ireland."[475]

Reflecting on the result, along with the passing of the Marriage Equality referendum in 2015, Máirín was elated. She had now moved from a society where she previously felt 'totally alienated... you can imagine my feelings when both referendums were passed and passed respectably.'

At the age of eighty, and after over sixty years of struggle, Máirín De Burca had finally arrived at what she called the 'final frontier'.

---

475 *The Irish Times,* 29th May 2018

20. A Remarkable Woman

How to sum up the life and work of a woman who has lived for over eight decades, much of it years full of activism and struggle? Máirín started her political life in 1954 and nearly seventy years later she is still engaged and involved.

Like everyone else there are different sides to Máirín. Various words come to mind to describe her. Activist? Certainly. Socially Concerned? Undoubtedly. Feminist? All through her life. Pacifist? From an early age. Fearless? Absolutely. Modest? To an extraordinary degree. Grumpy? Sometimes. Blunt? Often. Impulsive? Regularly. Scary? Yes, (but mainly to men). A loner? Yes. A woman with great friends? Also, yes.

Full Time Troublemaker

Máirín was once described as "a full time troublemaker" but also someone who was "so socially backward that she dreaded heading to a party with more than four people. Yet her belief in socialism was so strong that she thought nothing of taking on the great and the not so good and being flung behind bars for her trouble."[476]

---

476 *Irish Examiner*, 13th January 2011

The late Con Houlihan, a famed sports reporter with the *Evening Press*, once managed to weave Mary Robinson, Irish soccer manager Mick McCarthy and Máirín into the same article. Writing after Robinson was elected President, he described her as the "acceptable face of socialism", whereas Máirín he saw as "a great girl... who would have been happier in Paris in 1789 or in Barcelona in 1936."[477] Whatever about the 'great girl', Houlihan probably wasn't too wide of the mark. Máirín De Burca was a woman who always wanted to be at the centre of the battlefield.

Joan of Arc

People who worked with her and knew her well have used different words to describe her.

For Tony Heffernan Máirín was "like a coiled spring, carrying all the injustices of the world on her shoulders... she could be grumpy but also enormously charming." Her former 'boss' Pat Rabbitte saw her as a "remarkable woman. A once off and extraordinarily strong minded. She was determined to make a difference."

Des Geraghty, Máirín's colleague in many campaigns, saw Máirín as "the Joan of Arc of the working class." Fellow journalist and Sinn Féin colleague Padraig Yeates viewed her as "A tearaway... totally unintimidatable, a force of nature."

---

477 *Evening Press*, 14th November 1990

Eamonn Farrell, who campaigned with her in the DHAC, noticed that beneath all the 'in your face' protests Máirín was "quite a shy person." Similarly, her editor in *The Sunday Tribune*, Vincent Browne regarded Máirín as "a quiet presence in the office." Although that was probably one of the few times the words 'Máirín' and 'quiet' were put together. Pat Brennan, news editor at the *Tribune* and Máirín's ostensible 'boss' was very clear that "Máirín did not have a boss, never had a boss and never will have a boss and that's part of the wonder of her."

Máirín's colleagues in the IWLM were fulsome in their praise. Rosita Sweetman described her as "very serious and very determined... quite scary as well." For Margaret Gaj, Máirín was "one of the cleverest and most committed of all the women in the IWLM."

Not everyone had the same opinion, especially if they were on the other side of the barricade. The anonymous guard who spoke to *The Irish Times* reckoned that "if Miss De Burca was beaten at the Embassy she must have deserved it." The FBI reported back to Washington that Máirín was a "well known Militant Irish Extremist Left Winger.... the Republic's leading woman political agitator."

Her colleague from the DHAC, Hilary Boyle, challenged her after the Aldershot bombings in 1972. Máirín, she claimed, "became an accessory after the fact and as guilty as those who actually placed the bomb."

Far From a Saint

Máirín was far from being a saint. She could be blunt and diplomatic niceties were not her forte. At times she was a bit of a 'loose cannon' and on a whim she would head off with her pot of paint to daub some innocent telephone box (Ireland had lots of those back in the 'old days'). She seemed to be someone who needed to always protest about something, and it is debatable as to what all these protests actually achieved. But that was what campaigners did in the 1960s and 1970s.

And what is her own assessment? She is certainly a woman without regrets or complaints. 'There can't be regrets, because at the time there was no other choice… I am happy enough, I am a happy bunny at the way it went. I didn't expect to come into my 70s and 80s and get recognised for bits and bobs I did. And let's face it, they were bits and bobs. Ok, I will accept that the Juries Act was kind of important, it changed the law. But the others were bits and bobs.' Modesty personified.

Máirín is both philosophical and satisfied when she reflects on her long years of activism. 'Most of the stuff I did … they all led to change which is nice… I was pleased with the ending of the Vietnam war and apartheid. The Corpo (Dublin Corporation) even declared a housing emergency, though that didn't last long.'

No one could accuse Máirín of inflating her career and she is quick to point to the achievements of others, such as Mary McGee, a twenty-seven-year-old married woman with four children, who in 1973 won a case in the Supreme Court which found the ban on contraceptives to be unconstitutional. 'She changed the lives of half the population and a considerable number of the other half. What recognition did she get? Look at me, I got a degree. I keep getting invited to things… I have been over compensated and over recognised in my old age. How many people just fade into the background?'

Máirín at 80. A happy bunny. Photo. Derek Speirs

And personally? 'I was lucky in that I didn't want marriage or children. I never wanted children, but when I got older, I would have quite liked a grandchild, preferably a granddaughter, just one mind you … I am a happy bunny.'

And Finally

Three overarching themes stand out from all of Máirín's activism.

Firstly, she was always passionate in her concern for people who were disadvantaged or oppressed. Whether it was homeless people on the streets of Dublin, prisoners in our jails or black people in South Africa's townships, Máirín was a fearless advocate on their behalf. And she was a doer not just a talker. Yes, she could certainly speak and speak well, but she wanted to be doing things that made a difference. So, if she came across a homeless family it was a case of finding a vacant house and putting them into it. The fact that someone else owned the house was incidental. In Máirín's world actions always spoke louder than words.

Secondly, she was a feminist all of her life, long before that word became commonplace. Her involvement in the women's liberation movement was the most obvious example of this but she was always trying to see the world through the eyes of women, especially those who were struggling. Her involvement in the housing issue often led her to focus in on the mothers who were often, quite literally, left holding the baby, or babies.

And after her formal political career ended, she carried on writing and campaigning on women's issues – equality in the workplace, the introduction of divorce, the role of women in politics and the removal of the ban on abortion. Her achievement in getting the Juries Act changed is an enduring legacy. And on all of the other issues she campaigned on, Máirín saw different levels of progress in the course of her long career.

Finally, Máirín played an important role in encouraging her political party to move away from the use of physical force and to engage in non-violent methods in achieving change in the North. She was a fearless and brave critic of the Provisional IRA, even during the years when that was a risky thing to do. Through her efforts and the efforts of many others, Official Sinn Féin turned to democratic politics and moved leftward to tackle the many social issues Máirín was concerned about. That, in itself, was a significant change.

Máirín De Burca is a remarkable woman who has led a remarkable life, one full of conflict, struggle and achievement. It is a life which deserves to be acknowledged and celebrated.

And she isn't finished yet